Inside Manzano

Inside Manzano
The Life of a Nuclear Special Weapons Storage Site

CHARLES E. CABLER

McFarland & Company, Inc., Publishers
Jefferson, North Carolina

Disclaimer: This book is intended as a way to preserve the history of Manzano Base and to remember the military and civilian personnel who worked there during its 42 years of active service. The historical and military information in the book is derived from the public domain, declassified and published government sources, and information provided by government or private sources as reflected in the chapter notes and bibliography. A good faith attempt has been made to give credit for all information and photographs to the appropriate entity or individual, and permission has been obtained to use the personal stories and information in the book. The author does not guarantee the accuracy or completeness of these information sources. However, every effort has been made to provide the most factual information available. To the best of the author's knowledge and sincere belief, this book does not contain any classified information. It is not the intent of the author to represent, endorse, or promote the U.S. Air Force, Kirtland AFB, Sandia National Laboratories, any entity of the U.S. government, any private company, any individual, or any internet web site referenced in the book.

Frontispiece: United States Air Force, 1094th Aviation Depot Group emblem, created June 1955.

LIBRARY OF CONGRESS CATALOGUING-IN-PUBLICATION DATA

Names: Cabler, Charles E., author.
Title: Inside Manzano : the life of a nuclear special weapons storage site / Charles E. Cabler.
Description: Jefferson, North Carolina : McFarland & Company, Inc., Publishers, 2022 | Includes bibliographical references and index.
Identifiers: LCCN 2022034652 | ISBN 9781476688879 (paperback : acid free paper) ∞
ISBN 9781476646947 (ebook)
Subjects: LCSH: Kirtland Air Force Base (N.M.)—History. | Nuclear weapons—Storage—New Mexico—Kirtland Air Force Base—History. | BISAC: HISTORY / Military / Nuclear Warfare | HISTORY / United States / State & Local / Southwest (AZ, NM, OK, TX)
Classification: LCC UG634.5 K5 C33 2022 | DDC 358.4170978961—dc23/eng/20220727
LC record available at https://lccn.loc.gov/2022034652

BRITISH LIBRARY CATALOGUING DATA ARE AVAILABLE

ISBN (print) 978-1-4766-8887-9
ISBN (ebook) 978-1-4766-4694-7

© 2022 Charles E. Cabler. All rights reserved

No part of this book may be reproduced or transmitted in any form or by any means, electronic or mechanical, including photocopying or recording, or by any information storage and retrieval system, without permission in writing from the publisher.

Front and back cover photographs by Norio Hayakawa

Printed in the United States of America

McFarland & Company, Inc., Publishers
Box 611, Jefferson, North Carolina 28640
www.mcfarlandpub.com

1945
Gen. Henry H. "Hap" Arnold,
U.S. Joint Chiefs of Staff

"We must therefore secure our nation by developing and maintaining those weapons, forces, and techniques required to pose a warning to aggressors in order to deter them from launching a modern [atomic] devastating war."[1]

1961
John F. Kennedy, President, United States of America,
January 20, 1961, Inaugural Address

"Finally, to those nations who would make themselves our adversary, we offer not a pledge but a request: that both sides begin anew the quest for peace, before the dark powers of destruction unleashed by science engulf all humanity in planned, or accidental, self-destruction. We dare not tempt them with weakness. For only when our arms are sufficient beyond doubt can we be certain beyond doubt that they will never be employed."[2]

Table of Contents

Acknowledgments ix
Preface 1

Part I.
The Historical Development of Manzano

1. La Villa de Alburquerque, New Mexico — 6
2. Manzano Weapons Storage Site — 12
3. Sandia Base (Abbreviated History) — 21
4. Kirtland Air Force Base (Abbreviated History) — 27

Part II.
Manzano Begins, Code Name "Water Supply"

5. Site Able Construction — 34
6. 8460th Special Weapons Group — 39

Part III.
The Administrative Area

7. Access to Manzano Base — 44
8. The Administrative Area — 46

Part IV.
The Restricted "Q" Area

9. "Q" Area Access — 54
10. Nuclear Weapons Stored at Manzano — 57
11. Nuclear Weapon Storage Structures — 66
12. The Weapon Maintenance Plants — 74
13. The Birdcage for Pit Storage — 87

Table of Contents

Part V.
Base Security

14. DoD Nuclear Weapon Storage Area Security Program	92
15. Security Squadrons Responsible for Manzano	95
16. The Perimeter Fences	103
17. Storage Structure Security System	107
18. Central Security Control and ADT Monitoring	110
19. Patrolling the "Q" Area	114
20. Nuclear Weapon Convoy Duty	122

Part VI.
Miscellaneous Manzano Information

21. Aircraft Crashes at Manzano	134
22. Wildlife and Varmints on the Mountain	143
23. Manzano's Aerial Phenomena	146
24. Abandoned in Place	152
25. Kirtland Underground Munitions Maintenance and Storage Complex	162
26. The 377th Security Forces Squadron	167
27. Manzano Today	172
Epilogue	177
Appendix A. Aerial View of Manzano Base (Kirtland AFB)	180
Appendix B. Wall Map Displayed in the ADT Monitoring Room	182
Appendix C. Abbreviated Chronological History of Manzano	183
Appendix D. Manzano Base Commanders	188
Appendix E. Department of the Air Force Letter	189
Appendix F. Frequently Used Abbreviations and Acronyms	190
Chapter Notes	192
Bibliography	198
Index	199

Acknowledgments

Contributor Acknowledgments

In addition to an historical and a military and technical perspective, this book tells the inside story of the activities at Manzano. It can only be provided by people who were stationed at or associated with Manzano. There have been so many unique experiences on the mountain that attempting to single-handedly write this narrative would have been ineffectual. Therefore, I am truly grateful to the 15 officers and enlisted men who shared their personal stories and experiences from Manzano. All unattributed quotations within the book are from private interviews with these contributors, and as agreed, their identities have been removed to protect their privacy.

I appreciate the participation, cooperation, and patience of these contributors in the development of this book. Additionally, I express my profound appreciation to the individuals who not only contributed information but spent their valuable time reading and editing chapters or engaging in personal interviews. The book is a more factual and interesting read because of their participation. Each contributor provided personal experiences and anecdotes specific to his time on the base, therefore, his endorsement of all information in this book is neither stated nor implied.

Special Acknowledgments

My special thanks to Joseph T. Page II, a military historian and freelance and technical writer who provided a significant amount of assistance in documenting and validating the information in this book. His insight into historical writing was an inspiration, his substantial contributions were invaluable, and his generosity greatly appreciated.

Acknowledgments

I am indebted to Christopher McCune, the 377th Air Base Wing, Kirtland Air Force Base Historian, for his support. Chris graciously researched and provided historical documentation, general information, direction, and referrals to other individuals with knowledge about Manzano. I truly appreciate his interest in this project and thoughtful assistance to help me finish it.

I give special recognition to retired USAF Capt. Dave Coulie, who was instrumental in connecting me to all the contributors to this book. Dave was my first contact in attempting to locate personnel who were stationed at Manzano, and I soon discovered he knows most everyone in the Kirtland, Sandia and Manzano area. Dave, an AP since 1959, served two tours at Kirtland and is very familiar with the mountain. Dave is completing his 20th year as Chapter Chair, Pete Magwood Chapter, AF Security Forces Association. I appreciate his diligence and patience with me in my search for people.

Organization Acknowledgments

In addition to the contributors already listed, I am most grateful to the organizations listed below for providing information or assisting in locating research information. They were a tremendous help.

National Museum of Nuclear Science & History, Albuquerque, NM
U.S. Army Corps of Engineers Mobile, AL District, Research
USAF Police Alumni Association
AAir Aviation Archaeological Investigation and Research
Department of Defense National Archives
Special Interest Documentarian & Blogger

Preface

For most of us, being stationed at Manzano Base was just another change in duty stations during our enlistment. When we received our transfer orders, we had little idea of the significance of the base other than perhaps in concept, rumors, or information passed along to us. We certainly had limited to no understanding of the role New Mexico, Albuquerque, Kirtland AFB or Sandia Base played in the development of Manzano during the many events subsequent to the end of World War II. Such events include the Cold War, the Korean Conflict, the Cuban Missile Crisis, and the threat to the world posed by the nuclear arms buildup of the two world superpowers, the United States and the Soviet Union. Living in the reality of our assignment seemed to overshadow the importance of the history that had been or was being made at Manzano. Learning more about the history of the base, I now can appreciate my time there and have even more pride in serving at this base.

Site Able, as it was originally referred to before being renamed Manzano, was part of the Armed Forces Special Weapons Project and the first of six special nuclear weapons storage sites in the United States. When World War II's Manhattan Project was brought to a close, a new civilian Atomic Energy Commission was created as a follow-up organization. The Manhattan Project operations were moved to Sandia Base by the Atomic Energy Commission, and the Sandia Laboratories became the primary location for research, design, development, and testing of nuclear weapons. In 1959, the Armed Forces Special Weapons Project was reorganized and designated the Defense Atomic Support Agency and Sandia Base became the Headquarters Field Office Command.

As a subsidiary of Sandia, Site Able was constructed by the U.S. Army Corp of Engineers for the purpose of maintenance and storage of atomic and nuclear weapons under control of the Atomic Energy

Preface

Commission. Site Able became operational on April 4, 1950, and remained under the command of the Army until February 22, 1952, when control was turned over to the U.S. Air Force and the site was renamed Manzano. The Air Force maintained command of the base until its merger with Kirtland in 1971, and a partial list of Manzano Base Commanders is included in Appendix D. Through the rapid deployment capability of stored atomic and nuclear weapons, Manzano played an important role in nuclear war deterrence during the Cold War and long after. As a top secret installation, Manzano served the needs of the United States for 22 years before being deactivated as a weapons storage area. A new weapons storage area was developed at Kirtland, and all weapons were transferred from Manzano to the new location. Manzano was officially closed as a nuclear weapons storage site in 1992.

With its secret beginning, lack of traditional military base transparency, covert mission, and rumors of nuclear bombs, military and civilian people alike were curious about Manzano. The storage site was such a secret that most people in Albuquerque were aware only of the construction going on there, with little idea what was really transpiring. It wasn't until *The Denver Post* ran an article in August 1947, reporting the military was constructing a secret base with huge caverns for the purpose of storing atomic weapons, that people became aware of the base. *The Denver Post* identified the new base as being in the Manzano Mountains, southeast of Sandia Base. The military responded by issuing a statement that operations and construction near Sandia Base were top secret. The storage of nuclear weapons in Albuquerque has been a controversial issue since its beginning, and today, some 74 years later, the controversy continues. Fifty-five years after *The Denver Post* article, the Department of the Air Force continued to evade a clarification. A USAF memorandum dated December 30, 2002, states: "I can neither confirm or deny the presence of nuclear weapons or radioactive nuclear weapon components on Kirtland."[1]

This book, although highly abbreviated in content, documents Manzano starting with a high-level overview of Albuquerque's military history and the evolution of events over some 240 years that led to the creation of Manzano in 1946. Although the base was built some 75 years ago, the U.S. government continues to keep some secrets from that era under lock and key, as I discovered from the

Preface

denials of my Freedom of Information Act requests. All information within this book is based on declassified documents and publicly available information. The book is not intended to provide a complete chronological account of all historical events but only a snapshot composite of Manzano and the airmen who worked there.

While I identify myself as the author of this book, it contains not only many of my own personal encounters at Manzano but also a compilation of personal stories and experiences of several Air Force officers and enlisted personnel stationed there from 1953 through 1992. The book includes assorted photographs, maps, and descriptions in an attempt to answer the question asked by people for many years: "What really went on behind those Manzano security fences?"

If you were stationed at Manzano, I hope this book brings back good memories for you as it did for me and the contributors to the book and gives you a greater appreciation for the base and its significance. If you were never stationed at Manzano or never served in the military, I hope the book is written in such a way that it is easy to comprehend, despite the military and technical terminology. To this end, a page of frequently used abbreviations and acronyms is included as Appendix F for easy reference.

I hope you enjoy this historical, military and personal remembrance of Manzano.

PART I
The Historical Development of Manzano

1

La Villa de Alburquerque, New Mexico

Albuquerque, NM, is home to Kirtland Air Force Base, the largest installation in the Air Force Global Strike Command, Sandia Base, the principal nuclear installation of the United States, and its subsidiary installation Manzano Base, nestled in the Manzano Mountains southeast of Sandia Base.

Located nearby in Dona Ana County is the White Sands Missile Range, where the first atomic bomb, Trinity, was tested in July 1945. Albuquerque has been greatly shaped by the military occupation that occurred in New Mexico over time, and that military influence has been documented by several historians. Albuquerque has many times been referred to as the city of secrets. In the book *Trinity's Child*ren it was described this way: "It is a city that is driven by defense dollars, one where the military, and military weapons provide more employment in the city than any other industry. It is a city that, like so many of us, grew up with the bomb."[1] The city of Albuquerque and the state of New Mexico have played a significant military role for many years, and the history of Manzano is deeply entwined in both the state and city history. To fully appreciate this Manzano connection, a brief review of how Albuquerque began will set the stage to understand the vital role it played in American military history.

A Spanish charter was granted by Philip V in 1706 to establish the colonial outpost La Villa de Alburquerque (the original spelling). It was named for Don Francisco Fernández de la Cueva Enríquez, the 10th Duke of Alburquerque, Spain, and for many years, residents have referred to it as the Duke City. When it was chartered, the population of La Villa de Alburquerque numbered somewhere around 250. For 115 years the Villa de Alburquerque remained under

1. La Villa de Alburquerque, New Mexico

Spanish sovereignty until it passed to the country of Mexico in 1821. Because of its strategic location as a trading center and military outpost, Mexico found it advantageous to maintain a military presence in Albuquerque. Over time, the first "r" in its spelling was removed. The reason for the removal is unknown, although the difficulty in pronunciation has been suggested as the primary reason.[2] There the outpost remained until 1854, when the United States acquired from Mexico for $10 million through the Gadsden Purchase a 29,670-square-mile region consisting of present day southwestern New Mexico and southern Arizona and made it a U.S. territory. Albuquerque became New Mexico's largest city and home to several industries including uranium and coal mining. With the arrival of the Atchison, Topeka and Santa Fe Railway in 1880, Albuquerque became a major transportation hub along the Santa Fe trail.

With a population of some 2,500 people, Albuquerque was incorporated as a town in 1885 and as a city in 1891. New Mexico continued to be a U.S. territory until 1912, when it became the 47th state in the union.[3] Albuquerque was home to the Post of Albuquerque, a temporary U.S. Army Dragoon (cavalry) garrison post. After being abandoned, it was re-garrisoned in 1852, serving as a federal garrison and quartermaster depot. It would later be captured by the Confederate Army in 1862, with a gun battery set up in the town square (Old Town Plaza). Col. Henry Hopkins Sibley, the commander of Fort Union, New Mexico, resigned his U.S. Army commission, joined the Confederate Army and was promoted to the rank of general. Historians tell us that Gen. Sibley had difficulty making command decisions, perhaps partly influenced by his fondness of whiskey. In February 1862, the Confederate cavalry brigade under the command of Gen. Sibley occupied Albuquerque. When Col. Edward R.S. Canby and his small Union cavalry brigade advanced toward Albuquerque, he attempted to make a show of strength by ordering his four cannons to fire. The Confederates, located on a small hill near Old Town, returned fire. The battle for Albuquerque lasted only several hours, involved only the artillery, produced little physical damage and no casualties. Col. Canby issued an order for his men to stop firing, and the battle of Albuquerque was over with no apparent victory by either side.[4]

Albuquerque boasts the longest urban stretch of Route 66, otherwise referred to as the "Mother Road," created by the Bureau of

Part I—The Historical Development of Manzano

Public Roads in 1926, linking Chicago to Los Angeles. With the development of rail, road, and air transportation, Albuquerque's population continued to increase, recording 27,000 in 1930 U.S. Census and 36,000 in the 1940 U.S. Census.[5]

The first airport in Albuquerque was built in 1928 by two Santa Fe Railroad employees, Frank G. Speakman and William L. Franklin, using equipment loaned to them by the city. Two dirt runways were constructed; one, situated east-west, was 4,300 feet long, and the other, situated northeast-southwest, was 2,500 feet long. In a short time, the Albuquerque airport became a center of commercial aviation and as a crossroad for southwestern air traffic caught the attention of several air transportation entrepreneurs including James G. Oxnard in New York. Oxnard purchased William Franklin's interest in the new airport and named it Oxnard Field. Unfortunately, Oxnard Field was located close to the mountain range, giving many pilots concern about landing and takeoff safety. They registered several complaints and to resolve the problem a new West Mesa Airport was built in 1929, located a respectable distance from the mountains. Using the new airport was preferable for the pilots, and it began servicing all commercial air flights. Oxnard Field continued to operate but as a private airport.

During 1939, Army and Navy pilots discovered how convenient it was to use Oxnard Field for refueling and necessary maintenance. It was easy in and easy out, with little to no air traffic.[6] Recognizing the sustained use of the airfield and the potential benefits it provided, the Army acquired it, renamed it Albuquerque Army Air Base and restricted air traffic to military use. In late 1939, the Army leased land east of the new airport to set up a flight training base at the new location, leaving Oxnard to function separately. The first U.S. Army Air Force base commander, Col. Frank Hackett, assumed his duties in March 1941 and soon thereafter saw the arrival of the 19th Bombardment Group under the command of Lt. Col. Eugene L. Eubank, along with some 500 ground support personnel to help establish a definitive operating base. With the arrival of 2,195 bombardier and navigator trainees for the new B-17 Flying Fortress aircraft, permanent wood buildings began to replace the temporary Quonset huts, making life much better for the airmen stationed there. The new base began to take shape and look like a military facility.[7]

In February 1942, Albuquerque's Army Air Base was renamed

1. La Villa de Alburquerque, New Mexico

Albuquerque Army Air Base, April 28, 1942 (U.S. Air Force).

Kirtland Army Air Field in recognition of Col. Roy C. Kirtland, one of the first student pilots of the Wright Brothers and one of the Army's oldest pilots.[8] Throughout the war years, Kirtland Army Air Field continued to operate its flying, bombardier and mechanics training schools at full capacity, making great contributions to the war effort.

The Los Alamos National Laboratory, located a short distance northwest of Santa Fe, was initially organized during World War II as part of the Manhattan Project for the design and production of nuclear weapons. The nuclear-atomic bombs dropped on Hiroshima and Nagasaki, Japan, were developed at this laboratory under the leadership of Director Robert Oppenheimer. Dropping these bombs had a dramatic impact on New Mexico, which was little known at the time. World War II historian and author Nancy R. Bartlit writes in a recent newspaper article that the New Mexico 200th Coast Artillery Regiment had defended the Philippines until they were outnumbered and forced to surrender. After three years in captivity only about half

Part I—The Historical Development of Manzano

of those taken captive were still alive, and the Japanese war minister gave the order to kill all of them in the event Japan was invaded. However, the United States dropping these bombs convinced the minister that Japan was beaten, and the kill-all order was not carried out. Many New Mexico families were spared the loss of a family member as the result of the work performed at Los Alamos National Laboratory creating these nuclear bombs.[9]

Soon after the surrender of Japan in 1945, the B-29s of the 509th Composite Group, the group of Lt. Col. Paul Tibbets, pilot of the B-29 *Enola Gay*, left the Pacific Islands and re-established at the Roswell Army Air Base. This move made Roswell the first nuclear-bomber base and the 509th the first nuclear-strike force in the United States.

In June 1950, Albuquerque made national headlines after one of its residents, living at 209 North High Street, apartment number four, was arrested for being a Soviet spy. David Greenglass, brother to Ethel Rosenberg, was an Army sergeant working as a machinist on the Manhattan Project at the Los Alamos Laboratory. Mr. Greenglass, a Soviet spy code-named Bumblebee, hand drew plans from memory for the atomic bomb trigger mechanism and passed it to Soviet KGB courier Harry Gold. It is interesting to note that of the $500 Mr. Greenglass was paid for the drawing, he used $100 to purchase a U.S. war bond. Upon being arrested, Mr. Greenglass confessed to his espionage activities, agreed to testify against his sister and received a 15-year prison sentence. Today, this High Street house is listed in the downtown historic bed and breakfast area as the "Spy House."[10]

The city of secrets made espionage national headlines again in 2013, when a husband-and-wife spy team pleaded guilty to conspiring to violate the Atomic Energy Act and sell U.S. nuclear secrets. According to a *Washington Examiner* article published in June 2014, these two former employees of the Los Alamos Lab admitted to stealing and communicating classified nuclear weapons data to a person believed to be a Venezuelan government official. They had worked at the lab between 1979 and 2010. She had been employed as a technical writer and editor, and he worked as a physicist/scientist. According to court records, the couple had planned to help the Venezuelan president build a nuclear bomb and a secret underground nuclear reactor facility. This is interesting because, at that time, Venezuela possessed virtually no nuclear infrastructure or expertise and

1. La Villa de Alburquerque, New Mexico

was a member of the Treaty for the Prohibition of Nuclear Weapons in Latin America. The U.S. District Court judge in Albuquerque pronounced sentence on the two perpetrators.[11]

After the war ended, the Manhattan Project team realized the necessity of maintaining a nuclear stockpile of the war-time developed nuclear bomb, but where was the appropriate place to develop these bombs? The solution to their dilemma was to convert the old Oxnard field into a nuclear weapons facility, and it became designated as Sandia Base. For 25 years, from 1946 through 1971 when it merged with Kirtland AFB, Sandia was the primary nuclear weapons installation for the Department of Defense, functioning as a weapons research, design, development, fabrication, assembly, testing, and storage facility.

Once the bombs were created, the next problem to address was where to store the stockpile. The Armed Forces Special Weapons Project (AFSWP) was created and given the responsibility for all military functions relating to atomic energy, coordinating its activities with the Atomic Energy Commission. Lt. Gen. Leslie Groves, a United States Army Corps of Engineers officer who oversaw the construction of the Pentagon and directed the Manhattan Project, was placed in charge. The AFSWP chose and constructed the first storage site, identified as Site Able, located in the foothills of the Manzano Mountains, just east of Sandia Base in Albuquerque. On February 22, 1952, Site Able was renamed Manzano Base, and operations were turned over to the Air Force.

With this rich military history, New Mexico and Albuquerque can be proud of their contributions to our nation's freedom and national security. Manzano Base functioned independently from 1950 until 1971 when it, and Sandia Base, merged with Kirtland AFB. Manzano was home to many USAF and civilian personnel during its 21-year activation, and there are many stories to be told, several of which are included this book.

2

Manzano Weapons Storage Site

Manzano was a U.S. Air Force–operated installation located in the Manzano mountain range in Albuquerque, NM, just south of Sandia Base. It occupies part of the old Four Hills ranch, which was in the area prior to its purchase by the U.S. government, and sections of rustic, sagging fence still remain as evidence of the ranch's existence. This small mountain range, positioned north-south and approximately 30 miles in length, occupies the southern part of the larger Sandia mountain range. The Manzano Peak, the highest point of the mountain range, reaches just over 10,000 feet, equivalent to the Sandia Crest and South Sandia Peak.

The Manzano mountain range area was inhabited by several different groups of Pueblo Indians, including the Isleta Pueblo, until the late 1870s. In 1996, nine American Indian communities remained in the Manzano area, and in 2020, Native Americans in the Albuquerque-Manzano area represented 4.74 percent of the total population. Initially the region was a farming community, and sheepherding became the primary, non-farming occupation. In fact, at one point in time, Albuquerque was known as the sheepherding center of the West.[1]

The word "Manzano" translated from the Spanish language means apple tree. The mountains were given that name for the many apple trees planted in the nearby small town of Manzano. According to the New Mexico Bureau of Geology and Mineral Resources, legend is these apple trees were planted in the 1800s by Spanish missionaries traveling through the area to the Pueblo Indians. The few trees still remaining are possibly the oldest apple trees in the United States. Legend also has it that the Gran Quivira, the largest of three Spanish mission churches in this area, hid 1,600 burro loads of gold

2. Manzano Weapons Storage Site

Manzano mountain range (private collection).

and silver in the southern part of the Manzano Mountains, possibly in the Four Hills area.[2, 3]

Manzano Base begins to factor into the picture when the quest to show military superiority dramatically changed after the United States dropped the nuclear-atomic bombs on Japan in 1945. Since then, several countries developed a desire to have nuclear bombs in their array of military weapons. The Soviet Union's primary challenge to reach nuclear capability came to fruition in August 1949, when they tested their first nuclear weapon, a duplicate of the Fat Man bomb dropped on Nagasaki, partly developed from information supplied by Mr. Greenglass and other U.S. spies. After their successful test, the arms race between the United States and the Soviet Union was on.

To maintain a balance of power during the succeeding years of the Cold War and beyond, both countries built and stored massive numbers of nuclear weapons. This, they anticipated, would help ensure a condition of peace was maintained between these two nations through the fear of use and/or retaliation. Army Chief of Staff Gen. Maxwell D. Taylor, in his address to the U.S. House of Representatives in 1959, said: "The nation had enough nuclear weapons in its strategic force to annihilate the enemy ten times over."[4] There was, however, grave concern by politicians that the United States was placing too much reliance on the use of atomic bombs and the delivery capabilities of the Strategic Air Command. In 1949 a committee was formed to investigate this concern. It concluded that the atomic bomb was the most effective weapon in the U.S. arsenal and there was a need to mass produce these bombs.

To go a step further, Lewis Strauss, a member of the Atomic Energy Commission, stated in his letter to President Truman, dated November 25, 1949, "I believe the United States must be as completely armed as any possible enemy. I recommend that the President direct the Atomic Energy Commission to proceed with the thermonuclear bomb."[5] This anticipated massive arms buildup created the need for special weapons storage areas, such as Manzano, and the need to store them in a highly secured location.

Although Manzano was not a part of the Air Force when originally constructed in 1946, it was the first location developed as a national nuclear Weapons Storage Site (WSA) and fulfilled that function from 1950 until 1971. The photo in Appendix A provides an aerial perspective of the layout of the Manzano WSA, indicating the administrative and storage areas. The history of Manzano is intrinsically linked to both Sandia Base and Kirtland Army Air Field, dating back to the Manhattan Project in World War II, and the circumstances and events leading up to its development are interesting, beginning with the Manhattan Project.

The Manhattan Atomic Bomb Project

The discovery of nuclear fission by German chemists Otto Hahn and Fritz Strassmann in 1938 proposed that it was theoretically possible to create a bomb using uranium, producing a destruction force greater than anything known at that time.[6] In August 1939, U.S. physicists Albert Einstein and Leo Szilard, immigrants to the United States from Germany and Hungary, respectively, sent a letter to President Roosevelt advising him of the possibility of developing an atomic bomb and alerting him that Germany could already be working on such a weapon. Upon receipt of the letter and advice of military leaders, the president ordered the Advisory Committee on Uranium to begin a research project.[7]

Intrigued by the possibility of an atomic bomb, and encouraged by the Department of Defense (DoD), on June 28, 1941, President

2. Manzano Weapons Storage Site

Roosevelt signed Executive Order 8807 creating the Office of Scientific Research and Development with the power to engage in research and large engineering projects. With the additional research, investigations, and discussions, President Roosevelt approved the atomic bomb program in October 1941, which would eventually create the Manhattan Project. The president selected the Army to oversee the project rather than the Navy because the Army had more experience with management of large-scale construction projects.

Knowing the British atomic project, code named Tube Alloys, was in its infancy, the president agreed to coordinate the U.S. project with the British and sent a message to Prime Minister Winston Churchill, suggesting that they collaborate on atomic matters. The British and Americans exchanged some information, but because of the expense involved, the British were not aggressive in combining their efforts. With information about British budget limitations, President Roosevelt dispatched a letter to Prime Minister Churchill, offering to fund all research and development in the project. Unfortunately, the offer was poorly received, and Churchill did not even reply to the letter. As a result of the lack of interest shown by the British, the United States decided in April 1942 that its offer had been rejected and the better course of action was to proceed alone.

In July 1942, Sir John Anderson, the minister responsible for the British atomic project, advised the prime minister that they could make a real contribution in a joint project at that time, but a delay might render them unable to do so in the future. After considering that Great Britain's future to a great degree was inextricably connected to the United States and the possibility of a fleeting opportunity to participate with an ally, Churchill accepted the offer, and later that month he and Roosevelt made an informal, unwritten but solid agreement for atomic project collaboration. The formal Manhattan Project was authorized by President Roosevelt on December 28, 1942, in anticipation of ever-increasing war needs in what appeared to be a long-term war.[8]

The Manhattan Project, under the direction of Maj. Gen. Leslie Groves, U.S. Army Corp of Engineers, was noted for producing the first atomic-nuclear bomb during World War II. The Los Alamos Laboratory became an active part of the project in 1943, with much of the project work performed at Sandia Laboratories. The first nuclear device ever detonated was an implosion-type bomb

Part I—The Historical Development of Manzano

tested at New Mexico's Alamogordo Bombing and Gunnery Range on July 16, 1945. With Japan's refusal to surrender, on August 6, 1945, the United States dropped an atomic bomb on Hiroshima, followed by a second bomb on Nagasaki three days later, effectively ending the war. The Manhattan Project had fulfilled its objective to create the atomic bomb, and its work was done. The passage of the Atomic Energy Act in 1946 wrapped up the Manhattan Project and the Manhattan Engineering District and established a civilian Atomic Energy Commission (AEC) for a follow-up organization as the United States prepared to enter the new world of atomic energy. Through courage and dedication, Gen. Groves had accomplished his assigned mission. With the victory won, he turned the project over to his successors at the newly formed AEC and in his farewell address said, "Five years ago, the idea of Atomic Power was only a dream. You have made that dream a reality.... You built the weapon which ended the War and thereby saved countless American lives. With regard to peacetime applications, you have raised the curtain on vistas of a new world."[9] Gen. Groves would later say, "The atomic bomb made war unendurable, and its very existence makes war unthinkable."[10] The general consensus of opinion was that war is an imperfect instrument for conflict resolution and an armed forces response is often the only means to a satisfactory conclusion.

The Atomic Energy Act created a government monopoly on atomic energy, and along with defining governmental powers, it placed restrictions and penalties for the private creation or use of atomic energy without permission. Even the authors of the act admitted that it was a revolutionary piece of legislation for the time. Never before in U.S. peacetime history had Congress established an oversight agency with the extensive authority and responsibility given to the AEC. It included the provision to protect against the unlawful dissemination of restricted data and to safeguard facilities, equipment, materials, and other property of the commission, and it stated the president shall have authority to utilize the services of any government agency to the extent he may deem necessary or desirable.[11] This provision laid the ground work for the creation of Manzano Base.

The success of the atomic bomb was undeniable, and after World War II ended, increasing the manufacturing and retention of these weapons was determined to be a necessity. To improve the functionality and achieve the desired goal of mass production, command and oversight changed from the Army Corp of Engineers to a newly created Armed Forces Special Weapons Project (AFSWP), under the supervision of the AEC. This inter-service command was created by a joint letter of the secretaries of war and the navy on January 19, 1947, and was given the responsibility for all military functions relating to atomic energy, in coordination with the AEC. Headquarters for the AFSWP was assigned to Kirtland AFB in December 1949, and working with other Air Force agencies, its primary focus was on the future development of special weapons.

Kirtland became part of the Air Research and Development Command (ARDC) for the purpose of creating, testing, and analyzing weapons delivered by aircraft. The ARDC Work was a joint effort involving not only Kirtland but also the Atomic Energy Commission, Sandia Laboratories, and the Los Alamos Laboratory. The Air Force remained the focal point of the AFSWP and ARDC in great part because of its ability to deliver an atomic bomb most anywhere in the world on a short notice. With a continued interest in the nuclear program, in 1949 the Navy stationed a Naval Air Detachment at Kirtland to include its participation in the nuclear program and improve the Navy's nuclear delivery capacity.[12]

Manufacturing and Storing Nuclear Weapons

The atomic weapons developed in the Manhattan Project were individually handcrafted at the Los Alamos Laboratory, and because of wartime pressure, many desirable features to improve the weapon's efficiency were unachievable. The fission weapon, commonly referred to as the atomic bomb, had proven to be a superior weapon, and most people were of the opinion it was the weapon of the future. For such weapons to be mass produced, significant improvements were required in development, assembly, safety, and reliability. However, there were two major obstacles to overcome: the ability to manufacture and the proper storage of the weapons.

The manufacturing process posed the first problem. Throughout the war years, Director Oppenheimer continued to recruit physicists, chemists, metallurgists and explosive experts for the Los Alamos Laboratory. The facility, originally intended to house 30 scientists,

Part I—The Historical Development of Manzano

swelled to more than 6,000 residents at the height of the war. With the bombing of Hiroshima and Nagasaki prompting the surrender of Japan, the Manhattan Project mission to end the war through the use of atomic weapons had accomplished its goal. Although the war had ended, the AEC made the decision to continue manufacturing atomic bombs, and that presented a significant problem for the director. Many scientists and technicians recruited for the Manhattan Project desired to return to their home states and their civilian jobs, but the Corp of Engineers desperately wanted to retain these people for the future of nuclear weapon development. To appease this group of scientist and technicians, and retain the ability to manufacture weapons, Gen. Groves decided to relocate the weapons production and assembly activities from Los Alamos to another location, Oxnard Field in Albuquerque, New Mexico, into what would eventually become Sandia Base. In the summer of 1947, the Joint Committee on Atomic Energy met to discuss how many atomic bombs were required to ensure the national defense. Considering the number of predetermined Soviet targets and the expected bombing errors, the decision was made that 100 bombs were needed; then the number was doubled to account for a 50 percent plane loss during the attack.

The storage of these weapons posed the second problem. Many people were of the opinion that the storage location should be separate from the manufacturing location and that conclusion ultimately prevailed. The AEC and AFSWP, with the primary responsibility for the nation's nuclear stockpile, knew frequent maintenance requirements of these early atomic weapons required a specialized complex. Although the Army had several secure locations, the pressing question was: Were these located in an area close enough to the Z Division? Did they possess the ability to adequately protect the weapons from an attack, espionage or perhaps sabotage? The answer was no. There was little confidence in any location or the security programs, and it was becoming apparent that more than one storage location would be necessary to accommodate the number of weapons that would be manufactured.

After considering several possibilities, the first site selected as a Special Weapons Storage location was identified as "Site Able," just outside Sandia Base in the foothills of the Manzano mountain range, consisting of some 2,880 acres. The Corp of Engineers began construction in 1946 and Site Able became operational in April 1950.

2. Manzano Weapons Storage Site

The site was originally referred to as a "Q Area," because the AEC required a "Q" security clearance for all military personnel and civilian contractors needing access into the restricted area. This was an intense type security clearance involving, among other investigative scrutiny, a full-scale FBI background check. The Sandia Corporation was given the management authority of all Q Areas until 1952, when the Air Force was given that responsibility. The name was changed from Site Able to Manzano in February 1952, and it was placed under the command of the Air Force as the 1094th Special Reporting Group.

Although closely associated in the work process, Manzano was under a separate command from Sandia and Kirtland. Manzano was operated by the Air Material Command (AMC), and the nuclear components of the weapons were under the custody of the Atomic Energy Commission (AEC) and only released to the Air Force under strictly controlled protocols. In addition to AMC and AEC personnel, Sandia National staff members were on-site at Manzano to perform the actual maintenance operations and to instruct Air Force personnel.

The Armed Forces Special Weapons Project (AFSWP) was a joint organization, staffed by the Army, Navy, and Air Force, working closely with the AEC in the design, development, testing, production and storage of nuclear weapons, and command responsibility was placed on a rotation basis among these military services. The Defense Reorganization Act was signed by President Eisenhower in August 1958, increasing the authority of the Secretary of Defense. As part of this act, the secretary was authorized to establish such defense agencies as he thought necessary to provide for more effective, efficient and economical administration and operation. The first field agency established under the act was the Defense Atomic Support Agency (DASA) on May 1, 1959, which replaced the AFSWP.

An air policeman stationed at Manzano in 1953 stated, "Although this was an Air Force facility, the first year or so, we used Army weapons, drove 1952–54 Army pickups, were fed Army chow and were paid the Army way, once a month. The Sandia Base Commanding Officer was a Navy Admiral, and Sandia was managed by Western Electric. All our activities were coordinated by the AEC. At times none of us felt we were in the Air Force." That perception remained true over time. In 1964, those of us stationed there said

Part I—The Historical Development of Manzano

we were Army built, Air Force trained, DASA supervised, and Navy commanded.

Manzano continued to function as a top-secret nuclear weapons storage site, and even after 52 years, the Department of the Air Force has continued to refuse to officially acknowledge the existence of it or Kirtland as a nuclear weapons storage site, as indicated in the copy of a 2002 Air Force letter in Appendix E. In 1964–1966, Albuquerque residents were familiar with the Kirtland and Sandia bases, but very few even knew that Manzano existed, much less what went on there. Although several storage structures are visible to campers in nearby Coyote Canyon, Manzano was always inaccessible to unauthorized personnel. Metal signs were attached to the outside perimeter fence advising it was unlawful to enter the area without permission. A former Albuquerque resident indicated that when he was gowning up in Albuquerque, the phone book had a page with information on the three bases: Sandia (Army), Kirtland (Air Force) and Manzano (classified ordnance storage depot).

Manzano was operational until 1971, when a decision was made to consolidate Sandia, Manzano and Kirtland, all of which were associated with the nuclear program. The merger was concurrent with the change of DASA into the Defense Nuclear Agency and the Air Force's assumption of the primary responsibility for the nation's military nuclear weapons program. An abbreviated chronological history of Manzano is included in Appendix C. To fully understand the importance and mission of Manzano, it is beneficial to know about its parent bases, Sandia and Kirtland, both of which were interconnected in the operation of the Manzano nuclear weapons storage site. The following chapters provide an abbreviated history of those bases to demonstrate this interconnection.

3

Sandia Base (Abbreviated History)

Sometime after 1939, the U.S. Army purchased the original Albuquerque airport, named Oxnard Air Field, and transformed it into Sandia Base. For 25 years (1946 to 1971) Sandia, and its subsidiary installation, Manzano Base, was the DoD principal nuclear weapons installation with a primary function of weapon development, maintenance and storage. Sandia was designed to continue atomic weapons research, design, development, and testing started by the Manhattan Project during World War II. Here is how that occurred.

Within the Manhattan Project was an engineering group designated as the "Z Division," which needed to work in close proximity to the military for maximum development and testing results. With the shutdown of the Manhattan Project, the atomic bomb engineering and final weapons assembly work, carried out by the Z Division, was transferred to the Los Alamos laboratory in New Mexico. However, by midyear 1945 the lab began to experience a shortage of buildings and employees' accommodations. With space becoming unmanageable at the Los Alamos Laboratory, the Army Corp of Engineers acquired permission to convert Oxnard Field into Sandia Base, which would eventually become the nation's principal nuclear weapons installation. In 1947, Sandia Base became the permanent home for the Z Division's 147 engineers, the group that created the atomic bomb.[1] After the move to Sandia Base, the Z Division became a separate branch of Los Alamos Laboratory, and on April 1, 1948, it was named Sandia National Laboratories.

The majority of the Manhattan Project scientists, technicians and engineers were retained to work at Sandia, and Robert Oppenheimer, a University of California–Berkeley physics professor and

Part I—The Historical Development of Manzano

Sandia Base security gate, late 1940s (United States Department of Energy, Wikimedia Commons).

director of Los Alamos Laboratory, was instrumental in convincing the University of California to also manage the new Sandia National Laboratories. Agreeing to do so, the University of California managed Sandia from July 1945 until 1949, when President Harry Truman asked Western Electric, a subsidiary of American Telephone and Telegraph (AT&T), to assume the operations responsibilities. The Sandia Corporation, a wholly owned subsidiary of Western Electric, was formed on October 5, 1949, and, on November 1, 1949, assumed the management of the Sandia National Laboratories.[2]

To ensure the transfer and continuation of the military functions of the closed Manhattan Engineering District, in 1947 Secretary of War Robert Patterson and Secretary of the Navy James Forrestal created the Armed Forces Special Weapons Project (AFSWP), which was to work in coordination with the AEC. The AFSWP was re-named the Defense Atomic Support Agency (DASA) in 1959, and Sandia Base was designated as DASA Headquarters

3. Sandia Base (Abbreviated History)

Sandia National Laboratories Building 800, 1949 (*Sandia National Laboratories: A History of Exceptional Service in the National Interest*, 1997, p. 37, Wikimedia).

Field Command. Over the next 12 years, the Field Command was shared by Army, Navy, and Air Force officers on a rotation basis, and because of the presence of the AFSWP and its successors, Sandia Base had a strong representation of military personnel from all service branches, in addition to DoD and civilian employees.[3]

In 1971, DASA was once again revamped and designated the Defense Nuclear Agency and all nuclear weapon activities continued to remain at Sandia Base. As part of the DASA reorganization, Sandia, along with its subsidiary, Manzano Base, was merged into Kirtland Air Force Base, and the Air Force assumed responsibilities for the nation's military nuclear weapons program.

In 1996, DASA returned to its original role and renamed the Defense Special Weapons Agency (DSWA) without any change of mission or functions. DSWA was abolished two years later on October 1, 1998, and its responsibility and function transferred to the newly established Defense Threat Reduction Agency (DTRA).

As a government-owned, contractor-operated facility, Sandia National Laboratories (SNL) became the largest organization on Sandia Base. Its primary function was to design, develop, test,

Part I—The Historical Development of Manzano

and evaluate the components required to arm, fuze, and detonate a nuclear weapon, and to maintain the weapons systems integration programs to deliver the weapon to its target.

When the United States was actively developing nuclear weapons, the weapons were typically retired when they reached about 10 years of age and were replaced with new weapons. Because the United States is no longer designing new nuclear weapons or weapon systems, scientists, engineers, and technicians utilize a stockpile surveillance program to inspect and assess each nuclear weapon system periodically. SNL, in its stewardship role, became responsible for creating sophisticated tests and computer models to qualify those systems in the stockpile surveillance program. To ensure effectiveness, the life extension program tests individual components and refurbishes components nearing the end of their life through remanufacturing or redesigning as needed. This life extension program ensures the weapons remain safe and reliable and function as intended. SNL is part of that program, developing as much as 90 percent of a weapon system's 3,000–6,500 non-nuclear components.[4] SNL manufactures the specialized neutron generators and, as a backup, ensures the capability of producing batteries and high-explosive components. Once refurbished weapons re-enter the stockpile, Sandia conducts ongoing tests to assure the systems continue to meet requirements as they age. SNL operates several test locations, and the old Manzano Base is one of them.[5]

Located at Kirtland, Sandia National Laboratories remains active as a long-term research, development, testing and evaluation site. It is operated and managed by National Technology and Engineering Solutions of Sandia, LLC., a wholly owned subsidiary of Honeywell International, Inc. For 70 years Sandia has provided solutions for the United States' challenging security problems, and its goal is to remain the nation's prominent science and engineering laboratory for national security and technology innovation. Sandia functions as a federally funded research and development center today and continues to expand into new research, such as renewable energy sources. The Sandia technological and scientific research and developmental work assists in meeting several critical needs of the United States, as defined in a March 2006 Radiation Releases at Sandia National Laboratories/New Mexico report. Among those needs are

3. Sandia Base (Abbreviated History)

- maintaining the U.S. nuclear weapons stockpile in a safe, secure, reliable way;
- supporting a process of number of nuclear weapons reduction commensurate with U.S. Nonproliferation agreements and treaties;
- promoting the process of maintaining U.S. military strength through technology;
- protecting the U.S. from outside forces seeking to do harm; and
- developing a sustainable internal energy and information infrastructure.[6]

SNL supports the U.S. Department of Defense programs through national security related work to keep nuclear materials secure, confirm compliance with treaties, surveil foreign weapons systems and technologies, and oversee safe management of nuclear waste.

Today, what remains of Sandia Base is the eastern part of Kirtland AFB, and much of it is still recognizable from the 1971 merger. Many upgrades have been made over time; the old family housing was torn down and more modern units were constructed, and a new commissary and base exchange were added for convenience within the area.[7] The number of personnel employed at SNL in 2019 was approximately 12,300 people, with a $3.8 billion annual operating

Sandia National Laboratories, undated photograph (U.S. Air Force).

Part I—The Historical Development of Manzano

Sunset on the Sandia Mountains, taken from Kirtland Air Force Base (Anthony J. Bentley, 2013, Wikimedia Commons).

budget. An additional $2 billion for weapons activities at Sandia was included in the 2020 fiscal year budget.[8]

A former resident of Albuquerque told me that as the sun shines on the different rock formations, trees and vegetation, the Sandia mountains appear to change colors throughout the day, starting with a light-colored yellow-orange in the early morning and changing to a darker green at mid-day. But, the most impressive time to her is the late afternoon, when the mountains appear pink to a very pale red in color. She described them as beautiful. I often wondered why the mountains were named Sandia, until she told me, the Spanish word for watermelon is "Sandia." Now I know.

4

Kirtland Air Force Base (Abbreviated History)

Manzano Base is linked to Kirtland AFB through its connection with Sandia Base and the Armed Forces Special Weapons Program. Kirtland is the story of three bases, Kirtland Field, Sandia Base, and Manzano Base, brought together under one command in 1971, and has an interesting and diverse history. Command responsibility for Kirtland has changed many times over its 80-year history, but it remains as focused on training today as it did in 1941 when it began, and this abbreviated history reflects only a small portion of all that activity. There are several information sources, which provide more complete historical and technical information, but for the purpose of this book, this overview of Kirtland is included only to demonstrate the connection between it and Manzano Base. The Albuquerque Municipal Airport opened in 1939 with two paved runways. Shortly thereafter, the U.S. Army leased 2,000 acres from the City of Albuquerque near the airport for the Albuquerque Army Air Base, which was to later become Kirtland. Construction for base buildings at the new Albuquerque Army Air Base began in January 1941, with the firm of Morgan and Shufflebarger under contract to build 110 buildings designed to house 225 officers and 1,970 enlisted men, at a cost of $1,455,401. On March 8, 1941, the base was activated as a training center under the jurisdiction of the Army Air Corps (AAC) West Coast Training Center, headquartered at Moffett Field, in California. The base continued to expand as a training facility and during 1941, the bombardier school in Louisiana closed and the 19th Bombardment Group was relocated to the Albuquerque Army Air Base.[1] In February 1942, the base was renamed Kirtland Field in honor of Col. Roy C. Kirtland, an early Army aviator who, in 1912, became famous for piloting the first airplane from which a machine gun was fired.[2]

Part I—The Historical Development of Manzano

Throughout World War II, Kirtland functioned as a major training facility for bombardiers, aviation mechanics, and glider pilots. It is estimated that by 1945, some 5,719 students had received training at the base. Kirtland was instrumental in ending World War II by training the B-29 pilots and bombardiers who dropped the atomic bombs on Hiroshima and Nagasaki. After the war was over, the need to train massive numbers of bombardiers and aviation mechanics diminished substantially, and Kirtland Field was put on a stand-by status, pending a final decision about its future. The Army revived Kirtland Field in 1946, assigning it to the U.S. Army Air Force Air Materiel Command, an assignment that didn't last long. In 1947 the Air Force was created as a separate branch of the military by the Department of Defense Reorganization Act, and Kirtland Field was acquired by the new Air Force and renamed Kirtland Air Force Base (AFB) in 1948.

With its independence, the role of the postwar Air Force had to be defined. The Finletter Commission in 1948 suggested a new concept of airpower. A powerful peacetime force with the capability to counter any enemy air attack. The substance of the report in combination with the salesmanship of Generals Jimmy Doolittle and Donald Putt convinced the Air Force Chief of Staff to put the research and development mission on a more equal footing with the operational Air Force mission. Consequently, on January 23, 1950, the Research and Development Command (RDC) came into existence, only to be re-designated the Air Research and Development Command (ARDC) eight months later as a separate organization devoted strictly to research and development.

A Convair B-36A Peacemaker at Kirtland, 1948 (Kirtland Air Force Base).

4. Kirtland Air Force Base (Abbreviated History)

The Armed Forces Special Weapons Program (AFSWP) was established at Kirtland in December 1949 with a goal to instruct personnel how to build nuclear bombs. As part of the AFSWP initiative, the biological and chemical weapons research at Wright Patterson Air Force Base in Dayton, Ohio, was also relocated to Kirtland. The 2761st Engineer Battalion was organized at Kirtland during this time, with part of the battalion responsible for security at the base and another part assisting with bomb assembly.

In 1952, Kirtland AFB was enlisted as part of the ARDC, with the primary mission of analyzing, creating, and testing weapons coupled with aircraft. This was a coordinated undertaking involving Kirtland, the Atomic Energy Commission, Sandia Laboratories, and Los Alamos Laboratory. In 1958, scientists at the Special Weapons Center constructed a simulator in an abandoned dining hall at Kirtland and started to simulate the effects of nuclear explosions with a purpose to strengthen nuclear missiles, missile sites, and aircraft against possible enemy attack. In 1963, an Air Force Weapons Laboratory was created at Kirtland to research nuclear weapons' power and effects and the vulnerability of United States weapons systems to nuclear attack.[3]

The Partial Test Ban Treaty created a significant slowdown in military flying activity at Kirtland, and, as a result, in 1963 the Air Force Systems Command transferred 1,242 acres of land, including runways, taxiways, and ramps, back to the city of Albuquerque. The command entered into an agreement with the city to lease the use of the runways and taxiways, agreeing to continue providing crash and fire protection for the joint military and commercial airfield.

As part of operational efficiencies, on July 1, 1971, the DoD merged Sandia Base and Manzano Base with Kirtland. Through this merger, Kirtland assumed the responsibility for the Manzano nuclear weapons storage site and the weapons development laboratory at Sandia. With the creation of the Kirtland Underground Munitions Maintenance and Storage Complex, which replaced Manzano, additional emphasis was placed on base security. Because the Air Force had the security responsibility for several other nuclear weapons storage sites, there was a need to establish uniformity in the process to protect these locations. In September 1979, the Air Force established the Office of Security Police at Kirtland with an objective to develop standard security operational policies and procedures

Part I—The Historical Development of Manzano

for all Air Force resources and classified information. The office remained at Kirtland until 1997 when it was relocated to Lackland Air Force Base, in Texas.

The 1606th Air Base Wing assumed operational control and management of Kirtland in 1977 and continued that role until 1991, when it was deactivated, and the responsibility was transferred to the newly activated 542nd Crew Training Wing. Base Command responsibility changed again in 1993, when the 377th Air Base Wing was re-activated and assumed responsibility for Kirtland under the oversight of the Air Force Materiel Command. The 377th Security Force Group was assigned the security duty. On October 1, 2015, the Air Force Global Strike Command assumed administration of Kirtland Air Force Base from the Air Force Materiel Command and remains in charge today.

The year 2006 was very dynamic for Kirtland, with the acquisition of two major operations: The Nuclear Weapons Center and the 498th Armament Systems Wing, which were activated to manage weapons system acquisition, modernization, and sustainment. Additionally, Kirtland expanded into the space age when the Air Force Space and Missile Systems Center activated the Space Development and Test Wing at Kirtland. Following a 2010 reorganization of the center, the Space Development and Test Wing underwent major restructuring and was re-designated as the Space Development and Test Directorate.

On June 14, 2016, the Kirtland Air Education and Training Command once again expanded its training focus by activating the U.S. Air Force Pararescue and Combat Rescue Officer School under the oversight of the 351st Battlefield Airman Training Squadron.

Kirtland continues to host the Air Force's Nuclear Weapons Center (NWC) and the Sandia National Laboratories. It is the largest nuclear weapons storage facility in the nation, and possibly the world, housing up to 2,500 warheads. As an NWC, its responsibilities include acquisition, modernization and sustainment of nuclear system programs for both the Department of Defense and the Department of Energy. It is operated by the 898th Munitions Squadron, which reports to Air Force Global Strike Command.

The basic goal of the Air Force is to protect the United States with a safe, secure, reliable, effective, and affordable long-range precision strike force. Kirtland is committed to support that goal by

4. Kirtland Air Force Base (Abbreviated History)

developing excellence in individual personnel and teams. Leaders at every level are charged to cultivate a culture of respect, be an encourager, promote professional growth, and develop team members within their command to their maximum potential. In his May 2019 address to the U.S. Senate Armed Services Committee, Subcommittee on Strategic Forces, Gen. Timothy M. Ray, Commander, Air Force Global Strike Command, made this statement: "Our Air Force remains the most powerful in the world thanks to the help from Congress, and the vision and courage of those who have gone before us, but we cannot be static in a world where the dynamics of power are shifting. Our work demands excellence, not perfection, and Airmen at every level are valued team members, working together to accomplish the mission. Authentic leaders encourage innovation, bold ideas, and better ways of going about our business. It will take teamwork to win tomorrow's fight and we are stronger together. We are on a good path and moving forward."[4]

Today, Kirtland AFB is the largest installation in the Air Force Global Strike Command, the third largest installation in the Air Force Material Command (AFMC), and the sixth largest base in the Air Force. The base occupies 51,558 acres and employs over 23,000 people, including more than 4,200 active duty and 1,000 National Guard, plus 3,200 part-time Reserve personnel.

What started at Manzano in 1950 continues at Kirtland in a much greater way.

Part II
Manzano Begins, Code Name "Water Supply"

5

Site Able Construction

After considering several potential sites, three locations were selected as Special Weapons Storage Sites; one in Albuquerque, New Mexico, one in Killeen, Texas, and another in Kentucky. The Albuquerque site, in the foothills of the Manzano mountain range, met a majority of the AEC requirements and it was located in close proximity to the Sandia National Laboratories and Kirtland AFB. It was a remote location with limited-controlled access, and the geological components of the mountain made it possible to carve out the storage tunnels relatively easy. The decision was made. The first weapons storage site would be built at Albuquerque and identified as "Site Able." With the commitment to construct several storage sites, the code name "Project 76" was given to the combined project on October 31, 1946. Unfortunately, that code name was compromised, and a new name, "Water Supply," was assigned on September 15, 1947, and marked classified.[1]

I found no information available, either publicly or through a FOIA request, concerning the decision-making process or the environmental and feasibility studies that were conducted for Site Able. According to the Air Force Historical Research Agency, these records remain classified and restricted from release even after 75 years.

To ensure adequate long-term storage of atomic bombs and components, the AEC and the DoD assigned the project management of Site Able to Sandia Base. During 1946, the Kansas City engineering firm of Black & Veatch was hired, at the recommendation of President Truman, for the work at the Los Alamos facility. Because of the success at Los Alamos, Sandia decided to contract with Black & Veatch to design and engineer the specialized facilities at Site Able, and the construction work would be done by the Albuquerque District of the U.S. Army Corps of Engineers. Over the years,

5. Site Able Construction

the Albuquerque District had gained notoriety by successfully completing every mission assigned to it, overcoming the typical logistics, deadlines, and political pandering obstacles. Additionally, the district had developed a reputation for having the design and construction expertise for different types of military installation projects and support facilities. Unfortunately, after the end of World War II, the 1946 cutback in defense spending for military work decreased building projects drastically, resulting in a significant district work force reduction. Because the district was fearful of being totally eliminated, the contract to build Site Able came as a relief and provided some reassurances for longer-term employment. The district was granted $10 million ($163 million adjusted to 2022 value by the CPI Inflation Calculator) to build Site Able under the Army's command.[2]

In 1946, mining and drilling equipment was moved into the Manzano mountains, construction workers were hired, and the work begun under a top-secret protocol; however, the secrecy of the construction project didn't last long. As previously indicated, partly because of its military history, Albuquerque was nicknamed the city of secrets, and this secret government construction project just added to the validation of that title. Many of the construction workers lived in Albuquerque or surrounding areas, and they were under a strict no-talk rule. To the district's dismay, that rule only served as a catalyst for local speculation and paranoia about what was going on behind those fences in the Manzano mountains, including speculation about UFOs and the housing of aliens. The original AEC and DoD cover story, publicized as "Project Water Supply,"[3] specified that Sandia Base's need for additional water supply had necessitated the construction, which involved excavating work on the mountain. While that sounded believable to many residents, in 1947 *The Denver Post* published an article about the Manzano project, alleging that the military was constructing a nuclear weapons storage facility. In response, the military issued a statement saying the activities at Manzano were classified top-secret, without any additional explanation. The military never officially acknowledged the nature of the activities at the base; in fact several letters of denial were sent.[4]

Under the supervision of the District Engineer, Col. Henry F. Hannis (April 1946–May 1948), construction workers drilled and cut out tunnels and vaults into the mountain, reinforcing them with concrete and steel, making them essentially blast proof. A heavy

Part II—Manzano Begins, Code Name "Water Supply"

A U.S. Army Corp of Engineers tunneling project. While the tunnel shown here is construction from the Blue Ridge Parkway, a similar method would have been used (National Park Service).

steel door was put in place to provide access to each tunnel. While stationed there, a book contributor became friends with one of the civilian employees who had worked as a miner on one of the tunnel crews. This employee told the story about another miner who found a small vein of gold and pursued it vigorously until his supervisor strongly suggested he return to tunnel digging. So much for finding the mother lode!

Wooden forms were built along the walls of the tunnel to hold the poured concrete in place until it set. On one occasion, this same would-be gold miner put a pair of boots in the poured concrete so they could be seen when the forms were removed. Suspecting a person had been trapped when the concrete was poured, workers used jackhammers to hammer out that section of the wall. The miners got a big laugh out of this practical joke, but it was probably a good

5. Site Able Construction

thing the supervisors never identified the person responsible. This construction project, like many others, was not without labor problems. At some point the construction workers became disgruntled and went on strike, demanding an increase in pay. After some time and several negotiations, the workers settled for a 25 cents per hour increase, bringing their hourly wage to $1.75.

The original plans called for the construction of 41 underground storage structure and two underground maintenance plants, along with support facilities, roads fences, and alarm systems. A total of 121 structures were to be built at Site Able, 41 of which were tunneled deep into the mountain, providing a significant amount of protection from an aircraft attack, and 80 structures were to be free-standing and covered with earth. Site Able was one of six initial U.S. nuclear storage facilities. The other locations were: Site Baker at Killeen, Texas (Gray Air Force Base); Site Charlie at Kentucky (Campbell Air Force Base); Site Dog at Bossier Base, Louisiana (Barksdale Air Force Base); Lake Mead Base, Nevada (Nellis Air Force Base); and Medina Base, Texas (Lackland Air Force Base). In total, 13 Special Weapons Storage Sites would be built in the United States between 1947 and 1956. Other identical special storage sites were constructed at overseas locations; during the Korean War (1950–1953) President Truman sent the first atomic bombs to Europe as the first step in deploying atomic bombs to 24 countries including Labrador, Spain, Great Britain, Belgium, Morocco, Greenland and others.

In the opinion of some people, building this many storage facilities seemed a bit aggressive at that time because one year after dropping the bomb on Hiroshima, the United States possessed only nine Fat Man type bombs. The Mark 4 was put into production in 1949, and during the following four years, 550 Mark 4 bombs were produced. Ten years later, the U.S. nuclear stockpile had grown to 12,298 weapons, of which 3,968 were in AEC custody, and the remaining 8,330 were held by the DoD. Site Able was the storage location for a significant number of these weapons.[5]

Needless to say, security within the construction site was tight, and workers functioned on a need-to-know basis. Research indicates that these construction workers were blindfolded and transported from an assembly point on Sandia base to the worksite. If there was a need for them to leave their worksite for any reason they were once again blindfolded until they reached the desired destination. In

Part II—Manzano Begins, Code Name "Water Supply"

doing so, no one knew anything beyond their immediate tunnel work site. To say this was a compartmentalized project would be a gross understatement.

By the end of 1946, construction company Black and Veatch had completed approximately 85 percent of the original storage structure design plans. Site Able became minimally operational in late 1949 and was the third site to be fully operational. Site Baker at Killeen Base, Texas, was the first nuclear storage site in the nation to become totally operational, in March 1948. Killeen was a 7,000-acre base built into the hills of Texas, often referred to as Seven Mile or Rattlesnake Mountain. Killeen, the prototype for Manzano, had tunnels carved into the mountain, had maintenance plants, and was surrounded by four security fences, one of which was electrified with some 48,000 volts of electricity. To ensure effective security operational procedure was in place at the time of opening, several of the AP personnel stationed at Killeen were transferred to Manzano between late 1951 and February 1952.

Site Charlie, at Fort Campbell, Kentucky, was the second site to become operational. Although Site Able was operational, it was not totally completed until 1961.[6]

6

8460th Special Weapons Group

The first group to occupy Site Able in 1950 was the U.S. Army's 8460th Special Weapons Group, formed on December 22, 1948, by Maj. Gen. Leslie Groves.

As the Manhattan Project came to a close at the end of World War II, Gen. Groves was not certain the project would retain the remaining few bombs on hand, which consisted of nine Mark 3 bombs. Consequently, he took the necessary action to preserve the research facilities at Los Alamos Laboratory and the ability to continue producing nuclear bombs. As part of that action, he created a special unit to produce and assemble the Fat Man type bomb used at Nagasaki. Gen. Groves wanted to ensure that in the event of another war, the Defense Department would have at its instant disposal a special unit trained and ready to assemble atomic weapons. The premise was that if a war between the United States and the Soviet Union occurred, the only satisfactory end result was a U.S. victory. To form the special unit, Gen. Groves convinced the War Department to approve a project known as Operation Sandstone and send personnel to Sandia Base, a defunct Army Air Force facility near Albuquerque, which was being used as a graveyard for several thousand planes waiting to be cut up for scrap.[1]

Gen. Groves selected Col. Gilbert M. Dorland as the unit's commander and Col. R. Potter Campbell, Jr., to serve as the executive officer. On August 19, 1946, the 2761st Engineer Battalion (special) was activated at Sandia consisting of a headquarters company, a security company (Company A), a bomb assembly company (Company B), and a radiological monitoring company (Company C), which never became fully functional. The authorized strength of the battalion included 70 officers, one warrant officer and 397

Part II—Manzano Begins, Code Name "Water Supply"

enlisted men. In an effort to reduce the amount of training required by workers, improve work coordination, and speed the bomb assembly process, Col. Doran developed separate teams involving the electrical, mechanical, and nuclear personnel to become specialists in their assigned work and work in an assembly type process. Through instructions and oversight by Los Alamos Laboratory's Ordnance Division technicians, the teams became proficient in the assembly of bombs.

Col. Dorland's 2761st Engineer Battalion was one of the first joint organizations within the armed forces, and it was re-designated the 8460th Special Weapons Group on December 22, 1948, by the DoD.[2] The 8455th Military Police Company provided the base security during the construction phase and into its operation start date in 1950 until the changeover to the Air Force in 1952. The 8455th had also provided the security for Site Baker at Killeen Base, Texas, while it was under construction. The 8455th was the only official military organization assigned to Site Baker.[3]

Operation Sandstone demonstrated that not only could weapons become more plentiful, their design could be considerably diverse. That operation's success prompted Maj. Gen. Kenneth D. Nichols, Chief AFSWP, to proclaim, "We should be thinking in terms of thousands of weapons rather than hundreds."[4] With the decision to mass produce weapons, the 2761st Engineer Battalion went into full scale manufacturing operation, creating the need for adequate storage facilities. Before the AEC took formal custody of all atomic weapons in early 1947, Gen. Groves had already developed a preliminary construction design for national storage sites. These sites would not only house the weapons stockpile but also provide better protection against an attack than the crude facilities at Los Alamos and Kirtland Field. The first weapons storage area, Site Able, had already been approved, and work was scheduled to begin in 1947. The creation of the Armed Forces Special Weapons Project launched Sandia Base into the atomic age. Weapon production continued and by July 1947, the U.S. total inventory increased to 13. The next design in weapons, the Mark 4, was introduced and put into production in 1949, and during the following four years, 550 Mark 4 bombs were created. By the end of 1954, the U.S. stockpile of nuclear weapons topped 1,703 and storage sites were in greater demand. In contrast, the estimated number of atomic weapons possessed by the Soviets was only 150.[5]

6. 8460th Special Weapons Group

The 1094th Special Reporting Group, ultimately responsible for Site Able at Manzano, had its beginning when a group of airmen completing their basic training at Lackland AFB were assigned to the First Provost Security Squadron, the first air force group assigned to Killeen Base at its opening in 1948. The Air Force 1094th Special Reporting Group was created in 1950, and the First Provost Security Squadron commander, Maj. H.D. Hoover, a transfer from the 1100th U.S. Air Force Special Reporting Group, became the first commanding officer.[6]

Beginning in late 1951, the entire 1094th Special Reporting Squadron was transferred from Killeen to Site Able in New Mexico, relieving the existing U.S. Army Military Police unit from its assignment. The 1094th Special Reporting Squadron performed the same duties as they did at Killeen Base. The transfer was complete on February 25, 1952, when Site Able was formally renamed Manzano Base. The 1094th Support Squadron continued in place until July 1, 1971, when Sandia and Manzano bases merged with Kirtland AFB.

Part III
The Administrative Area

7

Access to Manzano Base

Manzano Base is located at the south end of Sandia Base and is rather remote, with limited access or public activity. The Manzano mountains, bordered by Kirtland Air Force Base and the Isleta Pueblo Indian Reservation, are popular because they contain the Manzano Wilderness, comprised of nearly 37,000 acres and 64 miles of hiking trails. However, even with these amenities, the Manzanos are visited with much less frequency compared to the Sandia Mountains. The Coyote Canyon recreational camping area is on the Northeast side of Manzano Base and utilized more by military personnel than by civilians. The secure bunkers at Manzano are easily visible to people within the camping area, but the security fences prohibit access to the base. Additionally, the highly restricted Sandia National Laboratories' field technical testing facilities are located in the Coyote Canyon.

The single destination road from Sandia Base leading into Manzano was the only way in and the only way out, providing excellent controlled access and security for the movement of nuclear weapons into and out of the base. It was close to the Kirtland Air Base for facilitating weapon exchanges and, starting in 1965, close to the Sandia secure railhead, should a weapon be transported via rail.

The base entry gates at Sandia and Kirtland provided the first level of controlled access to Manzano. This was the customary Army and Air Force access-granting entrance to the base for permanent or temporary personnel, contractors, and visitors. These gates were manned 24/7 by Military Police at Sandia's Gibson and Wyoming gates and Air Police at Kirtland's Eubank, Maxwell, and Truman gates. Access to Manzano had to begin through one of these gates.

There was only one gate or entry control point to Manzano. This gate was manned by Air/Security Police on a 24/7/365 basis. A Pass and Badge Office was located just outside the gate, and any escorted

7. Access to Manzano Base

person was required to obtain a pass from this office for travel within the administrative area. These passes were good for one time only, and visitors were required to remain in the presence of their host at all times. As discussed in greater detail in Chapter Eight, permanently assigned personnel were issued a badge, which granted them access to the general base area and to the weapons storage area when required to discharge their duties. Personnel could drive their personal automobiles onto the base provided they were cleared through the Pass and Badge Office and issued a special decal, which was to be displayed on the windshield of the vehicle.

Manzano was a mysterious and intriguing place for most military personnel, and because it was a highly restricted area, special arrangements were necessary prior to any visit. A former captain and liaison to the munitions commander, a four-star general and commander of Air Force Logistics Command (AFLC), who controlled the Manzano assets, told this story:

> Flag officers frequently wanted to see the inside of the base and have a guided tour of the portals. Occasionally after a visit, a message would surface saying, "I got into the largest weapons storage without any problem." After seeing a few messages, the AFLC commander decided any future visits to the mountain would be coordinated with his command center. He phoned me direct and let me know that no one could visit unless they cleared it through AFLC.
>
> One day, I saw a message advising that a major general (MG) from Strategic Air Command (SAC) was coming to visit Manzano. I immediately had Wing Protocol send a message to SAC Headquarters reminding them that the general's visit had to be cleared through AFLC. Needless to say, the MG arrived without the necessary clearance, and I had the unenviable task of telling him his visit had not been cleared. Upon hearing this news, the MG said something to the effect, "You see these two stars, Captain?" "Yes, sir," I replied, "but the commander has four stars and he controls this facility." Much to the MG's dismay, he was not granted entry. The AFLC commander phoned me the following day saying I did good, and four stars always beats two stars. I sure was glad to hear that, because I thought my career might have come to an abrupt stop.

One of the provisions contained in the original DoD Nuclear Weapon Security Program, followed by the revised DoD Directive 5201–41, Criteria and Standards for Safeguarding Atomic Weapons, issued December 8, 1962, was preventing unauthorized access to a nuclear storage site. The controls put in place for access to Manzano base effectively complied with this provision.

8

The Administrative Area

Because of the covert function and activities, Manzano Base was a somewhat remote location with restricted access as previously discussed, and being stationed there could invoke a feeling of being quarantined. In 1964, the base consisted of some 300 Air Force, Sandia, and DASA permanently assigned personnel. The base was divided into two areas: the administrative or general area and the weapons storage area. The location of the administrative area in relation to the entire base is indicated on the map in Appendix A. The administrative area supported all the general base functions, was located outside the weapons storage area, and was surrounded by four chain link fences topped with barbed wire. Access to the administrative area was restricted to military personnel assigned to Manzano and their immediate family members, who were issued permanent badges and permitted access at any time without an escort. Access by civilian contractors, vendors providing the base with essential supplies, and other military personnel was controlled through the Pass and Badge Office on an as-needed basis.

A number of buildings were needed to support the base once it became active, and construction on these buildings began shortly after the weapons storage construction started in 1947. By the time the base became operational in 1950, several buildings were ready for use, including the headquarters building, enlisted men's housing, the dining hall, the base fire station, motor pool, and a variety of support facilities. A vehicle repair shop and an electronics maintenance shop were added in late 1950.

Sandia and Kirtland bases had other social and sports related amenities available for Manzano personnel, but using those facilities presented something of a dilemma. The AEC and the Armed Forces Special Weapons Project leaders preferred keeping Manzano base personnel segregated and limiting the amount of contact and

8. The Administrative Area

Administration area (Google Earth 2009).

association with off-base individuals as much as possible. Their fear was Manzano personnel could be targets of espionage and or subversion. Even though nuclear weapons were not being manufactured at Manzano, they were stored and maintained in a state of readiness, and through their work, Manzano personnel possessed information that could be of interest to adversaries. Therefore, providing on-base recreation and support facilities minimized the interaction between Manzano and other military and non-military personnel.

As the number of on-base personnel continued to increase, additional amenities were needed and larger buildings required. In 1954, a movie theater-classroom, a softball field, and a security police dog kennel were added, and 1956 brought new amenities of a dining hall, small library, gymnasium, bowling alley, swimming pool, and non-commissioned officers' club. A chapel, gas station, and maintenance shop followed in 1957, with the last addition of a crafts and auto shop built in 1960.

Being stationed at Manzano had both benefits and drawbacks. For example, you didn't have a great number of people at the pool at any given time, nor did you have to wait in line for a stall at the auto hobby shop to work on your car. However, if you wanted to

Part III—The Administrative Area

go to the credit union, for example, you had to find a way to get to Sandia or Kirtland, because there were no shuttle services between Manzano and these bases. The Air Force tried to make Manzano as accommodating as possible and, in my opinion, did a good job. The 1964 "Welcome to Manzano Base" booklet given to all new arrivals stated, "We have in the past and will continue to take pride in the part each individual play in making Manzano Base the outstanding DASA base. I hope that you will apply your utmost energy in accomplishing our assigned mission, programming your education development, and increasing your physical fitness by participating in the sports program during your assignment here."[1] The administrative area included the following buildings, which hold vivid memories for several book contributors, as evidenced by their stories.

Pass and Badge Office. This office was originally established at the main gate to issue permanent access badges and visitor passes and to register automobiles and firearms for permanently stationed personnel.

On Base Housing. Single airmen were originally located in a building near the chow hall, then moved into the newly constructed three-story building number 143. Married personnel were housed on Sandia Base.

Building 143. In addition to on-base housing, in 1955–1958 an arms room was originally located in the basement of this building where Air Police drew and returned their M-1 and .45 sidearms. At some point in time the armory was relocated inside the "Q" area. In 1964, Building 143 also housed a small base exchange, a laundry and cleaners, the mailroom, a barber shop, and a unit supply for checking out sports gear and camping, fishing and hunting equipment for short periods of time.

Headquarters Building. This building dates back to about 1950 and provided space for the base commander and administrative staff, a personnel office, and a legal office.

Base Chapel. The Manzano welcome booklet provided to me in 1964 stated the chapel was built in 1957 to be the chaplain's office and provide for Protestant religious services. A Protestant Men of the Chapel group was organized in 1960 and was one of the most active groups on base. Roman Catholic services were conducted at Sandia Base.

Because of limited assembly space on base, the chapel was

8. The Administrative Area

occasionally used as an auditorium to accommodate a special meeting. According to an A1C AP, while he was there, special Character Guidance training was conducted in the chapel for the Air Police Squadron. "We had a very musically talented airmen in our flight, and before the chaplain arrived, this airman decided to entertain us with a couple of jazz numbers on the organ." Needless to say, the chaplain was not appreciative of this young airman's abilities, but the group enjoyed it, even more than the training. The AP said the airman drove a pink and white 1955 Cadillac Coupe de Ville. With that type of music and automobile, perhaps the airman was an Elvis fan.

Medical and Dental Services. In 1955, these facilities were located in Building 143 on the first floor and were eventually relocated to the headquarters building. These services were open during normal duty hours, and any non-duty hour sickness or accident was referred to the hospital on Sandia base.

The medical services hold a special memory for me because on one occasion, the doctor removed a small cyst on the back of my neck and excused me from swing shift (1600 to 2400 hours) duty the next day. Unfortunately, the doctor failed to advise Security Operations of the excused duty, as he said he would. When my flight commander located me at my girlfriend's home the next afternoon, he was livid and ready to classify me as AWOL. Thank goodness the doctor cleared that up for me, but I came close to having a big problem.

Medical Dispensary. The dispensary was located in the medical services room in the headquarters building and remained open to base personnel during off-duty hours in case of emergency.

Dining Hall. The dining hall provided four meals per day (breakfast, lunch, dinner, and midnight chow) for military and civilian personnel. A former AP said the dining hall was very nice in 1955, and when they changed from Army chow to Air Force chow, it was excellent! Apparently, that quality did not change over time. During my time there in 1964, the food was excellent. A former 1960s director of security at Manzano stated, "We had, at one point, what was selected as the best chow hall in the USAF."

As on many other military bases, kitchen duty (KP) came around regularly for most of us. A Weapons Specialist book contributor said, "In 1953, civilian KPs were hired, but by the time their security clearance was granted, they quit. So, the ready source of KP

Part III—The Administrative Area

staff was enlisted personnel below the rank of A1C. I was promoted to A1C and delighted to be exempted from the KP duty, but unfortunately, it didn't last long. About a year before I was discharged, there was a shortage of A2C personnel, so A1C were put back on KP duty. Every two weeks, rain or shine, I was scheduled for KP. I got to know the cooks and was on great terms with most of them. I worked part time at a TV repair shop off-base, and when I was scheduled for duty, the cooks would bring their TV sets for me to fix. It was amazing, but it took me most of the entire day to change one tube!" He didn't get completely out of KP duty, but he lessened the impact quite a bit.

Things didn't change much from 1953 to 1964. We pulled KP on a regular basis also. My favorite was midnight chow, because there was a limited amount of clean-up to do and several cooks let me cook my own breakfast. Now, that was a real treat. Another AP said he didn't mind the KP duty and on his days off, he often pulled KP for the married guys for $20 per day to make a little extra money.

Arts and Crafts Facilities. This facility offered a variety of crafts, including woodworking, leather carving, photography, ceramics, and lapidary. It is not certain when this facility was added, but it was a relatively new addition to the base. When I left in 1966, a buddy of mine was making a solid body guitar from a piece of hickory wood and doing a good job.

Auto Hobby Shop. The shop provided space, tools and automotive experts for general auto work. In 1955, the auto shop was located at Sandia Base, according to one book contributor.

Officers' Club. Located in building 143, the Officers' Club was open daily, providing a place for relaxation.

Oasis Service Club. This enlisted personnel club was built in 1953 and staffed daily. It hosted entertainment activities and included a TV room, game rooms, and a ballroom for special occasions.

Physical Fitness Program. Personnel stationed at Manzano were encouraged to maintain good physical fitness by using the facilities provided on base. These facilities included a bowling alley, softball field, swimming pool, and tennis courts.

Competitive Sports. Sports were a large part of Manzano Base activities. In fact, historical records indicate that the 8455th Military Police Company assigned to Site Baker at Killeen Texas were very involved. Baseball, basketball, volleyball, softball, boxing, golf and bowling teams were organized to compete at Fort Hood. Indications

8. The Administrative Area

are they had good results with some outstanding performers on these teams. When this company was assigned to Manzano in 1948, they brought the desire to continue in sports activities with their new assignment.[2]

Participation in organized intra-mural softball, football and track competition was available for anyone so inclined. An A2C assigned to the Air Police Squadron in 1954 tells me, "When I got to Manzano, I heard Sandia had a flag football team and wanted to replace their inexperienced quarterback. As I watched them practice, their coach asked if I could do better, and I said, yeah, I thought so. I had four years of high school varsity football and one year college varsity, was selected All League, and was an Honorable Mention All-State Athlete in high school. Unfortunately, because I was stationed at Manzano, technically I could not play for Sandia. So, I went back to the base, talked to several officers at Manzano and Sandia, and got permission through Special Services to form a Manzano team. I captained the team, recruited about 16 really good guys, and conducted try-outs to see who could best fill the positions. We had an outstanding team, winning the intra-mural base championships in 1955 and 1956."

Ten years later, this program was still going strong. I played on the Manzano flag football team in 1964 and 1965 at the position of tight end. Our coach was a second lieutenant, fresh out of OCS, on his first assignment, and he coached us very well. We didn't win the championship either year, but it was a lot of fun and full of bruises. For those are not familiar with flag football, let me assure you from personal experience, the games are intense, with a great deal of person-to-person contact. This A2C said, "One year, I suffered a concussion during a game and spent overnight in the Sandia Base hospital."

The airman also said, "During 1954–1956, Manzano also had a track team made up of four guys from Manzano and four from Sandia. We traveled to various bases all around the Southwest and participated in a huge track meet at Fort Sam Houston, comprised of Army and Air Force athletes. I ran the 400-meter hurdles, and despite my many successful runs, hit the last hurdle and fell. There went third place. I enjoyed my sports activity at Manzano and had the honor to be selected Athlete of the Month in October 1956. During those years, we had several gifted athletes on the Manzano

Part III—The Administrative Area

team, including a javelin thrower who competed in the All-Service finals held in Kansas."

In addition to these on-base facilities, Manzano personnel had access to a number of service clubs, recreational facilities, commissaries, finance offices, and credit unions, and a library, at Sandia and Kirtland bases.

Part IV
The Restricted "Q" Area

9

"Q" Area Access

The Atomic Energy Act of 1946, sponsored by Senator Brien McMahon of Connecticut, was a joint development by World War II allies the United States, the United Kingdom, and Canada. The primary purpose of the act was to establish a uniform policy on the control and management of nuclear technology. One of the major provisions of the act was to mandate that management of all nuclear activities would be under the supervision of civilians rather than the military. The act was signed into law by President Truman, on August 1, 1946, to become effective January 1, 1947. Upon its effectiveness, the Atomic Energy Commission (AEC) was created to assume responsibility for the U.S. nuclear energy program from the wartime Manhattan Project. One criterion of the AEC Act focused on granting access to the area where nuclear weapons were stored. I located the DoD directive that established the standards for safeguarding atomic weapons.[1] This excerpt is extracted from the directive.

    1. One of the threats to atomic weapons is covert action by persons with approved access. Therefore, access to exclusion areas will be restricted to properly cleared personnel on a need-for access basis and the number of persons having such access will be kept to a minimum.

    2. Entrance control to exclusion and limited areas will be formalized and maintained in order to effect positive identification of personnel prior to admission. A form of badge-exchange augmented by personal recognition provides the best control.

    3. Access control procedures will ensure that access to complete atomic weapons will be accomplished only when two or more persons are present who are capable of detecting incorrect procedures with respect to the task to be performed. This rule

9. "Q" Area Access

shall not be applied so as to preclude a responsible officer from taking necessary emergency actions which in his judgement are required to reduce or eliminate hazards to life and property, provided such actions do not involve operational employment, launching of the weapon or release of custody to foreign nationals.

There was a single access gate into the weapons storage area or "Q" area, housing the nuclear storage structures and plants. The location of this gate is indicated on Appendix A. This gate was manned by the Air/Security Police on a 24/7 basis and controlled with a badge exchange process. Through this exchange process, the individual wanting access would exchange his/her Manzano badge for a special "Q" area badge, required to be worn while in the area. The special badge indicated the individual's authorization to enter a facility, such as a structure or plant. A 1094th AP stationed there in 1955 said, "Permanent access badges depended on your security clearance. A Confidential clearance got you on base and the ability to patrol inside the perimeter road. A Secret clearance got you into the 'Q' area and the ability to patrol with someone who had Top-Secret. A Top-secret clearance got you into all areas as well as guarding inside the plants."

One component of the act was controlling the access to all Nuclear Weapons Centers (NWC). The AEC immediately started to develop a security clearance protocol for people associated with the various components of the nuclear program. They began by drafting a Personnel Security Questionnaire to establish basic personal information on all employees. With the realization that people working in the program had different access needs, setting up separate access designations was prudent. In the haste to create these different security clearance designations, they adopted a simple approach. Using the letters "P," "S," and "Q" from the Personnel Security Questionnaire, they defined the access level, using the following criteria. The letter "P" was given to contractors requiring general access but no need to work in a restricted area. The "S" letter was assigned to frequent visitors to an NWC but no access to restricted data. The letter "Q" was awarded to all personnel who had a need for access to the restricted area and/or restricted data. The "Q" designation was the only one of the three that required a full FBI background investigation. Over time, the "P" and "S"

Part IV—The Restricted "Q" Area

designations were terminated, but the "Q" designation remained active.[2]

A Weapons Specialist said, "In 1953, numbers one, two, and three were not punched out on my Q Area badge, but 4 through 12 were punched out, indicating I did not have access into those areas. I do remember that one of the Nuclear Specialists from Sandia had only number four on his badge; therefore, he was not permitted into Plants number I, II, or III."

There are several locations within the Q area designated as "no-lone zones," simply meaning, no lone individual can be within the area at any time for any reason. These zones are clearly marked at internal entry control points, but no external signs are posted so as to permit identification of these areas by aircraft or enhanced visual capabilities. The DoD two-person concept is a key element in the nuclear security program, designed to minimize and detect opportunities for a lone individual to perform an incorrect act or unauthorized procedure on a nuclear weapon, nuclear weapon system, or critical component. The two-person team concept requires that a minimum of two authorized people be granted access to a weapon within a security area—and not just any two people, but two people who are familiar with the safety and security requirements of the task to be performed. Each person must be capable of detecting an incorrect or unauthorized act by their counterpart. All personnel are required to report a two-person concept violation if they detect that a lone individual in a no-lone zone has had the opportunity to tamper with or damage a nuclear weapon, nuclear weapon system, or critical component.[3]

10

Nuclear Weapons Stored at Manzano

Throughout the 1950s, 1960s, and 1970s, Manzano WSA had a significant role in the maintenance and storage of nuclear weapons, as the United States continued to build its nuclear arsenal. Realizing the Soviets' aggressive intentions, George Kennan, a U.S. diplomat and statesman, wrote, "The Soviet power is impervious to the logic of reasoning, and is highly sensitive to the logic of force."[1] To determine the strength of the Soviet Union's atomic weapon capability, compared to that of the United States, a study was commissioned by the Joint Chiefs. The subsequent report, issued June 9, 1950, by this Joint Ad Hoc Committee titled *The Effect of the Soviet Possession of Atomic Bombs on the Security of the United States*, included the following observation: "The maximum threat to the United States of Soviet possession of atomic bombs, is the possibility that the USSR, in a single-surprise attack on the US, and its foreign installations, could seriously limit the offensive capabilities of the US, possibly to a critical degree.... Since the USSR will have an increasing capacity to deliver bombs on target, if not prevented, the extent of destruction that the USSR could inflict on the US will depend primarily on the defense capabilities of the US."[2]

The United States did not want to find itself in a position of vulnerability because of a small nuclear weapon stockpile; therefore, the nuclear buildup began. According to historical records, in June 1946, the United States had nine Fat Man–type nuclear weapons, either assembled or components ready for assembly. That number increased to 13 bombs in 1947, to 1,169 in 1953, and, at the end of President Eisenhower's two terms in office (1953–1961), to 22,229, compared to the Soviets' 2,471.[3]

Once the nuclear bomb secret was made public, any nation with

Part IV—The Restricted "Q" Area

the knowledge, material and money had the opportunity to produce a nuclear weapon. That certainly included the Soviets. However, because of the technical difficulties associated with building a bomb, the United States thought it would be 10 to 15 years before the Soviets were successful. Little did the United States know that the Soviets had a lot of help, as atomic bomb information was passed to the Soviets from England, Canada, and even sources within the United States, such as David Greenglass and the Rosenbergs.

Perhaps one of the most notorious persons was Klaus Fuchs, a communist German nuclear physicist who fled Germany in 1933 after Hitler's rise to the chancellorship. Just before the German invasion of the Soviet Union in 1941, he was accepted to work on the British nuclear bomb project in England. Later that year he was recruited by the GRU, the acronym used as the most recognized identification for Soviet military intelligence. Klaus, codename Charles, arrived in New Mexico with other British scientists in 1944, as part of the Los Alamos Laboratory team to work on the original bomb. His involvement at Los Alamos was the connection Soviet intelligence had been searching for, assuring them of a greater degree of useable information. Over time, the valuable information he provided to his GRU contacts impressed Stalin, promoting the necessity of instituting a Soviet atomic project. Klaus not only worked in his specialty of theoretical physics, he also volunteered to be project historian, a position that provided him with information beyond his normal project contributions. Klaus continued his spy activity until 1949, when the FBI and British intelligence identified him as a Soviet agent. During questioning, he began to talk freely, and the complete story of the atomic spies began to surface. He implicated his contact, Harry Gold, who in turn implicated his contacts, the Greenglass couple, who named the Rosenbergs in the espionage scheme.[4]

Although the Soviets were not as advanced in bomb making as the United States, they were successful and acquired a substantial nuclear stockpile. Both the United States and the Soviet Union maintained a close watch on each other's ability to wage nuclear war, and any unusual event gave rise to action. For example, on Soviet Aviation Day, May 1955, the United States—despite its reconnaissance efforts—was astonished watching 28 Soviet Bison M-4 long range jet bombers fly over, each one capable of carrying a nuclear weapon. The CIA calculated that if the bomber was in mass production, the

10. Nuclear Weapons Stored at Manzano

Soviets would have 800 planes by 1960. This speculation created a monumental concern of a "bomber gap" between the Americans and the Soviets and prompted an increase in the defense spending budget. However, to be discovered the following year by a U-2 reconnaissance plane, this demonstration was just another Soviet Cold War hoax to deceive the United States. In fact, only 10 Bison bombers flew on the Soviet Aviation Day in 1955. Once out of view, the planes quickly turned around, regrouped, added eight additional planes, and flew past the review stand again. That maneuver gave the impression there were 28 long range, nuclear capable, Soviet bombers ready for use, and possibly more on the production line.

The bombs developed by the United States during World War II were simply a product of the environment in which they were created. They were not the best design Los Alamos could have produced, but they could be built and made ready for use most quickly. During the period from 1945 to 1991, the American stockpile of nuclear weapons reached its peak in 1966, with more than 32,000 warheads of 30 different types. The Soviet nuclear stockpile reached its peak of about 33,000 operational warheads in 1988, with an additional 10,000 previously deployed warheads that had been retired but not dismantled. Manzano served as the first U.S. storage area, and several different types of nuclear weapons were stored there during its 20 years of operation. A few of those weapons stored at Manzano are discussed in the following paragraphs.

According to research information, the first type of nuclear weapon stored at Manzano was the Mark (MK) 5,[5] the first lighter weight bomb produced by the United States, which became the first missile warhead. Working with the MK 4 test results, scientists discovered that increasing the number of thinner, individual explosive lens units made the implosion more effective and simultaneously decreased the size and weight of the bomb. Therefore, the MK 5 was designed to use 92 individual explosive lenses, instead of the 32 used in MK4 and the Fat Man. The MK 5 measured only 44 inches in diameter and weighed only 1.5 tons. Additionally, the yield of up to 120 kilotons using the new core design was some three times greater than the MK 4. In a 1951 test at the Nevada Test Site, a MK 5's 22 kiloton blast at 1,435 feet could be heard some 300 miles away in Los Angeles and Salt Lake City, some 500 miles away. The smaller size and weight of the MK 5 made it ideal for use as the primary nuclear

Part IV—The Restricted "Q" Area

Mark 5 nuclear weapon (National Museum of the USAF display, private collection).

trigger for the first thermonuclear hydrogen bombs. Two doors at the front opened where the pit or capsule, discussed in Chapter Thirteen, was installed into the bomb shortly before deployment. The MK 5 remained in service until the end of 1962.

The next weapon design, the MK 6, was also stored at Manzano. There were seven designs of the MK 6 produced from 1951 to 1955, with a total production of 1,100 bombs. The MK 6 was 61 inches in diameter, 128 inches long, and weighed between 7,600 and 8,500 pounds. It was a "select-a-yield" bomb, providing the option of an 8, 26, 80, 154, or 160 kiloton yield, as desired. Additionally, it was the first bomb that could be assembly-line produced with near precision and quality, and it was in service until 1962. The USAF aircrafts which carried the Mark 6 were the B-29, B-50, B-36B, B-47, and B-52.

The MK 18, introduced in March 1953, was basically the MK 6 with extra reactive material added to the pit. A Weapons Specialist said the MK 18 was stored at Manzano. With a design yield of 500 Kilotons, it was the highest yield fission bomb ever produced by the

10. Nuclear Weapons Stored at Manzano

Mark 6 nuclear weapon (National Museum of the USAF display, private collection).

United States. The MK 18 design used the 92-point implosion system. With a natural uranium neutron reflector layer, it had over four critical masses of fissile material in the core and was considered very unsafe. Even an accidental detonation of just one of the 92 detonator triggers would likely cause a significant kiloton energy yield. In fact, it was so unstable and volatile, an aluminum chain designed to absorb neutrons was placed in the fissile pit to reduce the risk of accidental high yield detonation and removed during the last steps of the arming sequence. In total, 90 MK 18s were manufactured and were replaced by thermonuclear weapons in the mid–1950s.

This post-war bomb was designed to be used by tactical aircraft including the Air Force F-86 Sabre and the Navy FJ-4 Fury. The MK 12 (torpedo) was significantly smaller in both size and weight compared to prior nuclear weapons. The overall diameter was only 22 inches, compared to the MK 7 which had a 30-inch diameter, weighed 1,100 to 1,200 pounds, and had a yield of 12 to 14 kilotons of TNT. Although not verified, it was speculated to have used

Part IV—The Restricted "Q" Area

Mark 12 nuclear weapon (U.S. Government).

a spherical implosion assembly, levitated pit, and 92-point detonation. In order to compensate for the efficiency lost using less explosives, Los Alamos increased the number of detonators, first to 60 and then to 92 (32+60). This allowed for a bomb that produced about the same yield in a smaller size than its contemporary 60-inch brother, the Mark 4. The MK 12 was built in 1954 and remained in service until 1962.

The MK 12 was the weapon used in the 1991 fictional book *The Sum of All Fears*, written by Tom Clancy,[6] and in 2002 Paramount Pictures[7] made it into motion picture with the same name starring Ben Affleck and Morgan Freeman.

As work continued developing the atomic bomb, in 1942, a group of Robert Oppenheimer-recruited physicists at the University of California begin studying thermonuclear fusion which, if successful, would dwarf the atomic explosion capability. Many of these physicists were convinced that a thermonuclear weapon not only could be developed but that its development was of future necessity. Unfortunately, this opinion created a divide within the scientific community. Other scientists opposed a thermonuclear project on moral grounds, while others were of the opinion that developmental time was not of the essence. It would be several years before the Soviet Union developed nuclear weapons, and therefore the United States had no immediate need for a thermonuclear weapon. That

10. Nuclear Weapons Stored at Manzano

Mark 17 hydrogen (thermonuclear) bomb (National Museum of the USAF display, private collection).

perception changed however, with the Soviet nuclear bomb test in August 1949 and increased the argument for the development of a thermonuclear bomb. Even after the Soviet bomb test, the United States had to develop the thermonuclear bomb in the face of military and political provocations at home and from the Soviet Union. With the use of the atomic bombs on Japan still fresh and highly controversial, the president made the decision to proceed with the development of the thermonuclear super bomb.

Gen. Hoyt S. Vandenberg, Air Force Chief of Staff, testified to the Congressional Joint Committee on Atomic Energy that the super bomb would make the strategic deterrent more effective, becoming the major weapon in the arsenal of Strategic Air Command. On January 31, 1950, President Harry Truman signed a presidential directive and publicly directed the AEC to develop the hydrogen bomb, stating, "It is part of my responsibility as Commander in Chief of the armed forces to see to it that our country is able to defend itself against any possible aggressor. Accordingly, I have directed the

Part IV—The Restricted "Q" Area

Atomic Energy Commission to continue its work on all forms of atomic weapons, including the so-called hydrogen or super bomb."[8] The expectation was use-capability in 1954. The importance of this decision was recognized in August 1953. Just nine months after the first U.S. hydrogen test, the Soviet Union announced the development of its own thermonuclear weapon and then conducted its first major hydrogen bomb test in November 1955.

Dr. Edwin Teller, a Hungarian-born American nuclear physicist, was assigned the task of producing the U.S. thermonuclear weapon, and he conducted the first test on September 2, 1952, in the South Pacific. This test involved a 10.4 megaton hydrogen bomb, which exceeded the power of the "Little Boy" dropped at Hiroshima by 700 times. In the opinion of several people, including USAF Maj. Gen. P.W. Clarkson, the test results were one of the most momentous events in the history of bomb development.

The MK 17 and MK 24 were the first mass-produced hydrogen bombs deployed by the United States. At 24 feet, eight inches in length, 61 inches in diameter, and 21 tons, they were the largest nuclear weapons ever put into service by the United States. The MK 17 and 24 were identical except for the design of their primary section. The MK 17 had a yield of 15 megatons of TNT, while the MK 24 had a yield of between 10 and 15 megatons. Between October 1954 and November 1955, a total of 200 MK 17s and 105 MK 24s were produced. They entered service in 1954 and were phased out by 1957.

A Weapons Specialist said, "Before Manzano Plant III became operational, we needed a secure place to work on the M17s. A location on Sandia Corp property was available, so we packed all our junk and moved to Sandia. We set up shop and ordered an MK 17 from the storage structure. When it arrived via a straddle carrier, the operator deposited the weapon in the work area and started to back out the door. Big Problem! The straddle carrier without the weight of the weapon was now too tall to clear the door. We packed everything up and returned to Manzano until Plant III, with its 20-foot-tall doors, was completed."

The specialist also said, "There was a company in Albuquerque called South Albuquerque Works, operated by the American Car & Foundry Industries, which was instrumental in manufacturing metal cases for some of the MK 17s. They had a 25-foot lathe which could turn the aluminum case." The South Albuquerque Works

10. Nuclear Weapons Stored at Manzano

continued to operate until 1966, when they began to transfer the large metal case manufacturing to an Oak Ridge, Tennessee, plant, and the smaller case manufacturing to a plant in Kansas City.

In addition to these weapons, the Weapons Specialist said other type weapons were stored at Manzano or came in for maintenance. He said he worked on several weapons including the MK 15, 18, 21, and 26 at Manzano. Although the United States has not produced a nuclear weapon since 1991, existing warheads continue to undergo extensive and costly "life extension" upgrades, resulting in a sustained modernized arsenal. According to the Nuclear Weapons Archive report, the U.S. nuclear stockpile is comprised of three levels of accessibility.

> *Operationally Deployed:* weapons and delivery systems are operationally combat ready
> *Active Stockpile:* weapons available for immediate use, irrespective of their operational deployment status
> *Inactive Reserve:* weapons not in functional condition, for immediate use

According to this August 2007 report, the total of U.S. weapons at all levels was 9,962 warheads.[9]

The Stockholm International Peace Research Institute reports the nine nuclear-armed countries—the United States, Russia, the United Kingdom, France, China, India, Pakistan, Israel and North Korea—possessed a combined estimate of 13,400 nuclear weapons at the start of 2020. This number represents a decreased combined number from 2019, due in part to the dismantlement of retired nuclear weapons by Russia and the United States.[10] However, the 5,800 nuclear warheads in the United States and the 6,375 in Russia together still represent over 90 percent of all global nuclear weapons. Future estimations of the total number of nuclear weapons in the world will be a bit more difficult because in 2019, the U.S. administration ended the practice of publicly disclosing the size of the U.S. stockpile.

The Manzano nuclear weapons maintenance and storage facility operated until 1971, when it was merged into Kirtland AFB. The weapons at Manzano were relocated to Kirtland for permanent storage. It was estimated that 2,092 warheads were stored at Manzano at the time of the merger.

11

Nuclear Weapon Storage Structures

The storage of weapons and pits occurred in facilities referred to as "Structures," also referred to as magazines or igloos, depending on the time period referenced. The structures were an integral component of the weapons storage site, which included all the facilities needed in the maintenance and storage of nuclear weapons. As nuclear weapons became more technologically advanced, the storage of weapons within a single facility or at an individual site became of great significance, creating the need for enhanced storage facilities with special accommodations. Specialized structures and buildings were erected to serve the mission-based storage and maintenance needs at each site. Many of these new storage structures were constructed for a particular type of nuclear weapon and were characterized by design uniformity and standardization in materials. Because the critical criterion for new construction to accommodate nuclear weapons was safety, structures were generally constructed of reinforced concrete. The newly-created Air Force was responsible for the management of several new storage sites, such as Manzano, and because of their lack of construction experience or knowledge, they relied heavily on the U.S. Army Corps of Engineers for most of the early construction projects. As a result, many of the facilities constructed at Air Force bases are similar to those constructed for the Army. The common exception compared to Army facilities is primarily in structures for the storage and maintenance of nuclear weapons.

The Manzano mountains provided an ideal location as a weapons storage site. The mountains were somewhat remote, and their size area provided ample space for creating several storage structures. These storage structures and free-standing buildings were

11. Nuclear Weapon Storage Structures

required to be designed to avoid or survive an enemy atomic attack, while simultaneously limiting any negative repercussion to surrounding communities. Three types of storage structures were built at Manzano, defined as B, C, and D, and each type was built for a specific purpose or to accommodate a specific type atomic or nuclear weapon. Originally, 41 type "D" structures were tunneled into the mountainside and 35 type "B" free-standing structures with concrete walls, roof, and floor were constructed. When construction was completed in 1961, a total of 122 weapon storage structures had been built.

As referenced in Chapter Five, these structures were designed by Black & Veatch, a Kansas City engineering firm founded in 1915 in Kansas City, Missouri, specialized in construction, consulting, engineering, and mining. Although the design generally followed the standard plans developed by the Army Corps of Engineers and were constructed in great numbers during World War II, the Manzano structures had two major differences. First, the design must protect any structure or plant close by. In the event the contents exploded, the main force of the blast must be directed upward through the roof of the magazine. To accomplish this objective, the crown of the structure was constructed with reinforced concrete only six inches thick, and the side walls gradually thickened to one-and-one-half feet at the foundation. The structures were designed to withstand the force of an explosion equivalent to 500,000 pounds of explosives in another structure 185 feet away.

Second, the structure must incorporate protection from lightning, static discharge, and fire. Although the structures were built in the granite mountainside, an extensive grounding system was still required, not only for protection from lightning strikes but also for safely grounding static electricity.

Individual pieces of reinforcing bar used in the construction of the shell were welded to each other, forming a Faraday cage. The cage was then grounded or connected to an underground wire that encircled the entire structure. A steel door was connected to the cage frame.[1]

A good ventilation system within the magazine was required to remove fumes while personnel were working inside and to aid in keeping the magazine dry. Because of the structure design, the only acceptable method of ventilation was the natural flow of air through the interior spaces. Louvered openings in the front of the magazine, an adjustable damper near the bottom of the door, and a roof vent in the rear provided adequate ventilation.

Each structure had a concrete apron, which extended from the structure to the access road for loading or unloading the weapon when necessary.

The Mark (MK) 5, discussed in Chapter Ten, was introduced in 1952 and was the first type nuclear weapon stored at Manzano. With a length of about 10 feet, a diameter of 44 inches and a total weight of 1.5 tons, moving the weapon using a forklift was a relatively easy task.[2] However, when the MK 17 arrived in 1954, moving it around produced a new set of problems. The MK 17 was 28 feet, eight inches long, 61 inches in diameter, and 21 tons. Because it was so much larger than the MK 5, railroad type tracks were added in the structure to facilitate moving the weapon. An electric dolly on the track was used to move the weapon from inside the structure onto the apron, then a straddle carrier would transport the weapon from the structure to the plant. About a third of the largest structures had inside track switching capability, so four MK 17s could be stored safely.

The different types of storage structures are shown and discussed on the following pages.[3]

The type B structures completed in 1950 were free-standing structures with a semi-circular concrete roof covered with earth and had vertical, sloping concrete walls. The structure was entered through a set of double steel doors into a tunnel that was 12 feet wide and 20 feet long. Opening the doors on this structure required more effort than other structures. When closed, the bottom of the doors dropped into a three-inch deep trough cut into the concrete, with a large hook fastened to the top of one leaf of the door, connected to a ring at the top of the door opening. To open the doors, a specially designed hydraulic jack was used to raise the door until it was high enough to clear and swing away from the trough and the ring. The procedure was reversed to close and seal the door.

Because the weapons in each structure were not accessed at regular intervals, a ventilation system was necessary to ensure there was no buildup of fumes and to aid in keeping the structure dry. The ventilation system consisted of small louvered openings sealed by an adjustable damper at the bottom of the door and a concrete vent

11. Nuclear Weapon Storage Structures

Type B structure (Sandia National Laboratories/Kirtland AFB).

through the roof, covered with a metal hood. This provided a constant flow of fresh air into the structure.

An additional type B structure had a second set of double steel doors, separating the tunnel from the storage area. Because of this distinction, it was often referred to as a "super igloo." It was larger with an overall length of 81 feet and contained approximately 2,146 square feet. The structure had several lighting rods to help defer any possible lightning strike.[4]

Type C structures were free standing structures consisting of two laboratory rooms, which were used to verify the continued viability of the nuclear core. The intensity of the nuclear core was periodically tested by exposing a radioactive source to the plutonium capsules. A Geiger counter would monitor and gauge the activity.

These structures were approximately 83 feet in length and slightly over 29 feet in width, providing a total of 2,432 square of feet of space. With double-leaf, steel-jack-type doors, front and rear ventilators, lightning protection, and drainage system, their

Part IV—The Restricted "Q" Area

construction was similar to other structures. Because of the type of activity conducted within this type of structure, it was designed to withstand an explosion within another structure up to 185 feet away, with an equivalent to 500,000 pounds of explosives. Because the face-wall of the structure was considered to be the weakest part, they were constructed of 18-inch-thick concrete from the foundation to the top of the door and 12-inch-thick concrete from the door to the top of the structure wall. For additional protection, a barricade of concrete and earth was often built opposite the door.

Forty-two type "C" structures were built in 1953. These structures were built to the east of Plant II in two parallel rows along an access road. It was, therefore, important to protect each individual structure from a problem occurring at another structure in close proximity. Should an explosion occur within the structure, it would no doubt be completely destroyed. However, by designing the structure to control the direction of the explosion, it would prohibit a chain-reaction destruction of nearby structures. Many type C structures were equipped with a floor safe to secure the testing sources. However, when the plutonium capsules were replaced with a sealed initiator in 1967, less testing and maintenance were required. Thereafter, the C structure was no longer needed for this purpose and became just a storage structure.[5]

Initially, 41 type D structures were tunneled into the mountain. Double steel doors, varying in height from 40 to over 100 feet, provided access to the entry tunnel. Another set of doors, requiring the use of a hydraulic jack, were located at the end of the tunnel, providing access to the storage area. The vertical sidewalls and arched roof of the access tunnel were constructed with reinforced concrete, and the 26-foot by 60-foot storage chamber was similar with an arched roof. Ventilators were installed with the vent opening extending outside the mountainside.

The structure required an extensive grounding system for protection not only from lightning strikes but also from static electricity. The reinforcing steel bars within the storage chamber walls were grounded to the surrounding rock with steel rods drilled into the rock or attached to steel plates. Eight-foot-long steel rods were drilled into the rock above the structure to disperse any lightning ground strike.[6]

11. Nuclear Weapon Storage Structures

Type A Structure

The increase in the numbers and types of atomic weapons and the accelerated maintenance schedule prompted the conversion of seven of the Type D structures into special storage referred to as "A" structures. Technically, there was an A structure as well as an A-2 structure, both identical in design. These 41-feet by 50-feet structures were built of reinforced concrete, and from a distance, the exterior gave the appearance of an office building. A central corridor, approximately eight feet wide, led to the interior storage space which was divided into four, single-entry cells with a narrow corridor between each pair.

Access to each cell was through a steel door, which opened with a single combination lock. Each cell was approximately nine feet by 30 feet and contained steel shelves as shown in the photo below. Atomic bomb detonator pits or capsules were housed in "bird cages," and these cages were stored on the steel shelves. One structure held 30 detonators in each room, for a total of 120 detonators. Booster

Steel shelving for storing birdcages (RCG&A).

capsules for the thermonuclear or hydrogen bomb were also stored in the type A-2 structures. The pit storage space in this structure is a berm or below ground, with a false single story of solid reinforced concrete above ground.[7]

Type S Structure

A different type of building was needed to maintain thermonuclear weapons, so the "S" structure was designed and built sometime after 1954. These irregularly shaped one-story, flat-roofed buildings had a structural system of reinforced concrete with concrete masonry unit walls, and the interior was separated into several work areas. To facilitate moving a weapon for assembly and disassembly, a 10-ton overhead crane was installed in the bay. The purpose of this type of structure was to supplement the quality control work by separating the routine maintenance and assembly functions performed in Plants I and II from other quality assurance activities. The S structure, also known as a surveillance structure, contained mechanical and electrical bays, a calibration room, and a photography laboratory. The quality assurance function was staffed by employees from Sandia Laboratories.[8]

After Russia developed and perfected a nuclear weapon, the threat of a nuclear confrontation during the Cold War became a greater concern. The United States continued to increase its nuclear weapon stockpile, and in 1958, the number increased to 7,345.[9] As the number of weapons increased, so did the storage requirements, and by the end of the 1950s, 13 storage locations had been developed. Manzano played an important role in housing a significant number of these weapons.

Although at one time it was necessary to store nuclear weapons only at special locations such as Manzano, today things have changed dramatically using a new Weapons Storage and Security System, WS3. Many weapons, such as the tactical B61 nuclear bomb, are now stored in a protective aircraft shelter floor vault, directly under the aircraft intended to carry the weapon. The location inside the aircraft shelter increases the weapon survivability in case of any kind of attack, and the hard lid and reinforced sidewalls of the vault provide ballistic protection. The WS3 has an electronic monitoring

11. Nuclear Weapon Storage Structures

protection process that utilizes sensors, electronic data-transmission and security equipment such as video, motion detectors, and closed circuit TV coupled with thermal imaging devices. The WS3 system was authorized in 1988, and was in widespread use by 1995.

Although the WS3 system provides for the safe storage of a weapon, there remains a significant need for a designated weapon storage facility as we will discuss in Chapter Twenty-Four. Weapons must undergo a periodic inspection and re-validation process, which takes place in the underground nuclear storage facility at Kirtland AFB. After that inspection process, the weapon can be delivered to a base using the WS3 system, ready for immediate deployment if needed.[10]

12

The Weapon Maintenance Plants

Initially, nuclear weapons were very large, could only be used as free fall bombs, and were referred to with a "Mark" (MK) designator. When Manzano became active in 1950, the first weapons stored there were the MK 5 and MK 6, first-generation atomic devices requiring assembly and ongoing interval maintenance. To provide these integral services, maintenance plants were constructed at Manzano. The first two plants constructed, designated as Plant I and Plant II, performed inspection and testing of weapons' sub-assemblies; testing of non-nuclear mechanical and electrical systems; and the maintenance of associated assemblies. Eventually, Plant III worked on the MK 15, 17, 24 and 36 weapons. The nuclear weapons specialists working in these plants were top grade people selected and trained by the DoD, as specified in the DoD security program excerpted below.

> SECTION 3: DOD NUCLEAR WEAPON SECURITY PROGRAM C. (U) Personnel. Personnel who are selected to perform nuclear weapon duties must demonstrate the highest levels of integrity and dependability. These personnel will be assigned to designated DoD Reliability Assurance Program (RAP) positions, or a host-nation equivalent, and will be evaluated for adherence to RAP standards, as described in DoD M 5210.42.

Because of the type and nature of the job, personnel assigned to work with nuclear weapons were given an extensive background check, as would be expected. Each candidate had to qualify for a DoD Top-Secret security clearance through a rigorous and very thorough screening process. This process involved a single scope background investigation (SSBI), requiring several weeks to complete. The SSBI scrutinized the candidate's personal conduct, medical history, legal background and finances. Any history of drug use, alcohol abuse, or

12. The Weapon Maintenance Plants

failure to pay personal obligations would likely result in a disqualification An SSBI can also be disconcerting to those involved in answering questions. One A1C Special Weapons Technician at Manzano stated, "One of the groups within the Atomic Energy Commission (AEC) was searching for qualified people. While at Keesler AFB, Mississippi, I and a few of my buddies were looking for an exciting job in the Air Force, so we decided to fill out their Personnel Security Questionnaire (PSQ). After hearing nothing about the PSQ, I forgot about it. Two months later I called home and my mother frantically asked me what kind of trouble I was in because the FBI was asking questions about me. I had no idea why the FBI was asking questions and pleaded innocent but wasn't sure whether or not she believed me. Anyway, shortly thereafter, I was notified of my Top-Secret Clearance, and after telling my mother, she was very pleased that I was not in trouble."

DoD candidates were also subject to the Personnel Reliability Program (PRP). This is an evaluation for anyone who handles or has access to biological, chemical, or nuclear weapons and is designed to ensure the highest possible standards of individual reliability in personnel performing duties associated with nuclear weapons and critical components. A candidate must demonstrate trustworthiness, be of good conduct, with total allegiance to the United States. The PRP requires the selection and retention of only those personnel who are emotionally stable, physically capable, and have demonstrated reliability and professional competence. Individuals who did not meet or maintain program standards would not be selected for or retained in the PRP or assigned any duty associated with nuclear weapons.

Even after being qualified initially, the performance and conduct of individuals subject to the PRP are continually evaluated. Although the program was never designed as a basis for punishment or disciplinary action, if an individual's conduct or reliability indicates a problem, they receive an immediate evaluation. If the evaluation conclusion requires action, there are three levels of disqualification that can be taken.

> *Suspension* is used for a period of time not to exceed 30 days which cannot be renewed/extended. This action removes the employee from duty without starting a formal decertification process. For example, an individual temporarily on some type of medication.

Part IV—The Restricted "Q" Area

Temporary Decertification This action is for a person who, for some reason, does not meet the program's standards. It normally extends for 180 days, but can extend in additional 30-day increments, not to exceed 270 days total. A typical example is when an individual is under investigation by the OSI/FBI.

Permanent Decertification is the permanent removal of an individual. For example, alcohol abuse or drug dependence.

An individual receiving any of these actions, even a permanently decertified action, can be reinstated in cases where there is sufficient justification that the disqualifying problem no longer exists and there is little likelihood the problem would not return under any stressful situations.[1]

After successfully passing these type investigations, a Nuclear Weapons Specialist Military Occupation Specialty code (MOS and later retitled AFSC) was awarded and weapons training began. The training was intense and lengthy. According to an A1C electrical technician candidate, the instructors were all well versed in their field of expertise and were experienced teachers. Typical training and tech schools for an electrician included (1) six months Electronic Fundamentals at Keesler AFB, (2) two months Assembly Basics Electrical at Sandia Base, (3) two months Assembly Functional Components Maintenance of the Major Components Radars at Sandia, and (4), for the highest graded Airmen, one month thermonuclear weapons maintenance at a remote location on Kirtland AFB. After the technical training was completed, permanent base assignment followed.

The first two plants, designed to assemble and provide maintenance on conventional and eventually thermonuclear bomb components, were located at Manzano. In anticipation of withstanding a 15- to 20-kiloton nuclear blast, Plants I and II were tunneled deep into the mountain. Plant I, completed in 1949, was located on the west face of the mountain, and Plant II, completed in 1950, was on the east face of the mountain.[2]

All facilities needed for maintenance of the weapons, inert storage, administrative areas, break and change rooms, emergency generators, and support facilities were located in these plants. The work areas and interconnecting tunnels were of reinforced concrete with

12. The Weapon Maintenance Plants

Plant I entry portal (Kirtland AFB and RCG&A).

vertical side walls and arched roofs, very similar in appearance to an earth-covered igloo. Special security measures were incorporated into the construction of the plants, including heavy bank-type metal vault doors. Initially, additional security was provided by each door having two combination locks, and no single person knew both combinations.

As indicated in the RCG&A blueprints, each plant had two entrances about 300 feet apart, comprised of two arms forming the letter H. Each arm was approximately 40 feet wide and 25 feet high, and extended some 1,000 feet into the mountain. At the end of each arm was a mechanical bay, with the electrical bay located between the back arms of the H. The mechanical bay and the electrical bay were about 200 feet long, 100 feet wide, and 30 feet high, and they were not connected to each other internally. Each bay had a two-inch copper strip anchored to the wall about three feet off the floor. This strip was intended to be slapped by all personnel upon entering to discharge any residual charge. Both plants had a tunnel on the right side of the entrance leading to the Nuclear Bays.

Security for the plants consisted of one guard at the portal entrance who checked the access badge of every person entering the portal and one guard at the entrance to the maintenance area. Although the personnel identification process worked well for the secured entrance, the vulnerability assessment initiative considered the plant ventilation system a major security weakness. The AEC required a ventilation system for each plant to ensure air was properly filtered prior to being discharged into the environment. These cylindrical vents, indicated with an arrow, are evident in the photo of Plant I above. In Plant II, where the maintenance of thermonuclear booster cylinders was performed, a special room vented tritium gas using a vacuum intake device through the ceiling of the

Part IV—The Restricted "Q" Area

plant. While functionally necessary, unfortunately, there were few ways to implement effective security mitigation strategies in the ventilation system.[3]

One story I came across in my research indicated the vent shafts were designed with a built-in ladder so plant personnel, bearing firearms, could climb up the shaft and out onto the mountain to help in any defensive action. If that story is true, the vents were adapted for that use after 1956 because a special weapons electrical technician stationed there in 1956 tells me, "Each bay had two or more vents to expel radioactive radon gas. Inside the plants, vents were in the ceiling at least 40 feet off the floor. There were no ladders up to the vents, and there were bars across the opening."

The blueprints do not indicate any connection between the two East side and West side plants. However, there has always been speculation that they were in fact, connected. A major in the 1608th SPS told me, "I searched every nook and cranny, trying to find the secret opening, but never found it." If there was a connection, it was well-hidden and has never been disclosed.

As the U.S. nuclear weapons arsenal continued to grow and with the introduction of thermonuclear weapons, it was soon realized that the existing plants could not accommodate future needs. The new bombs weighed as much as 44,000 pounds, requiring the construction of a third assembly and maintenance plant, Plant III. Working with nuclear weapons, the AEC gained knowledge through experience and realized neither Plant I nor Plant II would realistically survive a thermonuclear (TN) weapon blast. So there was little reason to tunnel the new plant into the mountain. The decision was made to build the new plant above ground as a free-standing building. With the construction started in 1953, this new plant would be designed to service thermonuclear neutron weapons. Unlike Plants I and II, where maintenance work was carried out in separate reinforced areas, the two maintenance bays of Plant III would not be sub-divided. Each bay was equipped with a large overhead crane, rated at 10 tons, and steel shelves were installed along the walls to hold the birdcages. Completed in 1955, this plant served the same purposes as Plants I and II but was limited to the disassembly and maintenance of newly stockpiled thermonuclear weapons.[4]

The year 1954 presented the need to add yet another free-standing plant, designated as Plant IV, which was completed in 1955

12. The Weapon Maintenance Plants

and also devoted to thermonuclear weapons. These irregularly shaped one-story, flat-roofed buildings used reinforced concrete for the structural system, with concrete and masonry walls, and were overlaid with a significant depth of earth.[5]

Plant III (Plant Kirtland AFB and RCG&A).

The work within the plants was continuous, routine, and always under strict oversight. This oversight was promulgated by an Atomic Energy Commission directive stating that a minimum of two authorized persons, each capable of detecting incorrect procedures with

Plant IV (Plant Kirtland AFB and RCG&A).

respect to tasks to be performed, and familiar with safety and security requirements, would be present during any operations requiring access to the weapon.[6] This procedure was deemed necessary in preventing an operational error or sabotage. A former weapons technician stated, "While working at plant number III, there was always an officer present while you worked on the weapon. Working in close proximity with the officers often created a friendship, which was highly discouraged by the AF major in charge of the plant, but it occurred anyway. Among those officers was a 1st Lt. Marvel, who was a good guy, but took a bit of ribbing when he was promoted to captain."

From the beginning, atomic bombs required periodic maintenance. For example, the combat readiness of the MK 3 Fat Man could be maintained for only a short period of time. Once charged and installed, the life of the lead-acid batteries was only nine days, and if the batteries were not removed, they would begin to corrode, rendering the bomb unstable. The complete dismantling and reassembling process took 40 technicians working up to 70 hours. In time, as the life expectancy was extended, the Air Force maintained a service record on all nuclear weapons, and twice a year each weapon was removed from its storage structure for inspection and maintenance and then returned to its storage structure. Weapons were delivered to Plants I and II on a Yale lowboy front loader by special weapons handlers and moved into a plant mechanical bay, where waiting electrical technicians removed the X unit and batteries, and transported them to the electrical bay. The X unit, the part that actually fires the detonators, was charged up to 2300V and discharged into a dummy load five or six times to confirm its functionality. The result of each discharge cycle test was recorded for future reference.

In the radar section of the electrical bay, the major components radars (MC) were inspected, cleaned and fully tested. A special weapons technician said, "All weapons did not include the same MC items on board. For example, the MC 1 in a MK 5 and MK 6 contained a klystron radar, a rather dangerous item to work on, which was eventually replaced by a magnetron radar. Each radar was programmed to detonate at a certain altitude, and if it failed to function, one of four MC barometer switches would close, causing the weapon to detonate." Needless to say, functionality testing was an indispensable process to ensure that an intact, unexploded, weapon did not fall into the hands of the enemy. In the later developed TN weapons, barometric sensors were the primary triggering device, so there was no radar in those weapons. The components radar cans were cleaned, repainted a stunning shade of olive drab, and relabeled with part numbers and the inspection date. All electrical parts and the MC radars were tested on equipment specially designed by the Sandia Corp.

In the mechanical bay, the weapon was disassembled, inspected, cleaned, diagnostics tested, reassembled, and their batteries recycled. Because a weapon was never permitted in the electrical bay, when the maintenance work was completed, the electrical technicians returned the tested components back to the mechanical bay

12. The Weapon Maintenance Plants

Diagnostic testing (National Archives, ARC# 76048736).

for reinstallation. The photo above, taken in 1945, is a Little Boy type weapon, hooked up to a diagnostic machine testing its components.

The average turnaround time in Plants I and II was about five days for a traditional nuclear weapon and about 14 days in Plant III because the TN weapon required much more mechanical work than the Fat Man type weapon. After all maintenance and inspections were completed, the weapon was returned to its structure or placed in Strategic Air Command (SAC) ready weapons storage area. When it was time for maintenance on a nuclear weapon housed at an outlying base, the weapon was flown into Kirtland AFB, removed from the aircraft by special weapons handlers, and transported to Manzano via truck under substantial security guard protection. One of the existing stock weapons was removed and exchanged for the weapon requiring maintenance.

Each mechanical bay had 25 personnel assigned to it, and they worked on only one weapon at a time. In the electrical bay, there were about 20 personnel working, contemporaneously supporting both mechanical bays. A special weapons electrical technician,

Part IV—The Restricted "Q" Area

stationed there in the 1950s, said, "I remember there was no smoking in the mechanical bays, but smoking was permitted in the electrical bay, so we always had a lot of wrench jockeys in our bay. The officer in charge of the plant was usually a captain, or major, and he stayed in the office, rarely ever came to the bays." I have been told that the AEC nuclear weapons technicians were kept separated from the electrical and mechanical weapons technicians. These AEC technicians were housed somewhere on Sandia Base, and as a general rule, the Manzano technicians did not even know their names. Perhaps this was a precautionary measure to discourage any possibility of the two groups collaborating and devising a plan to blow up the whole mountain with a nuclear blast.

Working around and inside these nuclear weapons, the potential of radiation always created anxiety and concern for all personnel. Exposure to high levels of radiation, such as being in close contact with a defective weapon, can cause acute health effects such as skin burns and acute radiation syndrome (radiation sickness). It can also result in long-term health problems such as cancer and cardiovascular disease. Radiation monitoring at the plants was always a concern; however, it appears that radiation safety was often an obfuscation. How much exposure to radiation was too much? In 1954, the military had no definition, so they adopted the industrial standard of 3.4 rads, the equivalent of three chest x-rays at that time. Anyone receiving this limit would be restricted to work in a safer place. In 1954, an Air Force officer said regarding radiation exposure, there was "rule safety" and "real safety."[7] This was evident in the response to the thermonuclear bomb tests conducted during Operation Castle in the Philippines in March 1954, when two test bombs detonated with over twice their predicted yields. One test in particular, Castle Bravo, produced such extensive radiological contamination it not only affected U.S. soldiers stationed there but nearby inhabited islands as well. This radiation fallout resulted in health problems for many of those exposed.

At the time of the Castle Bravo test, a Japanese fishing boat, the *Fukuryu Maru* (*Lucky Dragon*), was approximately 82 nautical miles from the test area and received a heavy dose of radioactive fallout.[8] When the *Fukuryu Maru* returned to its home port in Japan, the effects of the radiation exposure were severe enough that several crew members required hospitalization. Because of the American

12. The Weapon Maintenance Plants

and Japanese media reporting about the Castle incident, the general public was made aware, possibly for the first time, of the extended dangers of radioactive fallout.

The special weapons electrical technician said everyone inside the plants was required to wear a dosimeter, which was collected weekly by a safety officer to test the radiation exposure level of all personnel within the plant. The technician also said while he was stationed there, he never heard of a radiation leak at any of the plants. I would anticipate wearing a dosimeter would have always been a requirement for anyone working directly with the weapons or in close proximity. However, according to the wife of a weapons handler, stationed there in 1965–1967, he wasn't required to wear one. Perhaps as the weapons and pits became safer, and weapon handling procedures improved, wearing any type of radiation detection device became optional. Unfortunately, this weapons handler died in 2017 from aggressive prostate cancer. His wife tells me that it was never determined whether his cancer was attributed to his work at Manzano.

Job safety was always a major concern. With this much activity taking place within the plant, avoiding workplace hazards was very much a part of the everyday routine. However, even as cautious as personnel were instructed to be handling these weapons, accidents did occur. The electrical technician relates one such accident involving a truck inside the "Q" area. While transporting a MK 12 torpedo weapon up the hill to a storage structure, the pintle clamp, holding the front loop of the weapons drawbar, became disconnected from the truck. Apparently the locking clamp on the pintle assembly was not securely locked in place initially, and the weight of the MK 12 going up the hill forced it open. The weapon slid off the truck bed and rolled backwards down the hill, but it did not explode. Needless to say, the incident created a substantial amount of uncertainty for those working in the vicinity.

Another accident occurred in Plant III, while working on a MK 17 thermonuclear (TN) weapon. As part of the maintenance process, the front of the MK 17 was removed to gain access to the conventional mechanism used to trigger the TN weapon. In a specially designed rail system, the front of the M17 is bolted to a 75-pound spacer ring and a crank assembly is used to remove the weapon. The spacer ring is about four feet outside diameter and about 20 inches

Part IV—The Restricted "Q" Area

thick. It is placed on the rails, carefully pushed into place and bolted to the trigger weapon. Unfortunately, someone, without thinking, pushed on top of the spacer to get it into the correct position for extraction. It became unbalanced and tilted forward, crashing down on top of one of the 92 detonators. Fortunately, the smashed detonators did not explode the 5,000 pounds of high explosives inside the trigger device.

Within the plant's close quarters, any activity, whether a vehicle or person, must be a calculated movement and implemented with great caution. On another occasion inside Plant I, an inexperienced driver—attempting to navigate a flatbed truck loaded with a case of detonators—drove under a MK 6 weapon, crushing the box of detonators almost flat. Fortunately, the detonators survived the accident and did not explode. The driver was reassigned to the motor pool the next day.

During the early years of Manzano, the plants hosted many visitors and dignitaries. Air Force generals, high-level DoD and AEC people were regular visitors, and, surprisingly, a number of British military officers also made visits. These visiting dignitaries never identified themselves or who they worked for, but they all displayed green Top Secret Cleared badges. About every six months, SAC would call an alert, and the entire base would go on lock down or extended duty schedules.

There is an old saying in the military that if anything can go wrong, it will, and at the most inappropriate time. This next accident may very well have been the origin of that old saying, but thank goodness, it was able to be corrected. The base was alerted that a high-ranking government official, rumored to be the secretary of war, and a four-star AF general were planning to visit Plant III for a demonstration of the MK 17 TN weapon handling and inspection process. The official and his group assembled in the plant, the weapon was brought in, and the usual procedure initiated to begin the inspection process. The MK 17 was a 20-ton weapon with a marked center of gravity (CG) band around the middle to permit safe handling and loading into a B-36B aircraft. A "U" shaped mechanical handling device, approximately 40 feet long, was used to maneuver the weapon around. Unfortunately, during the previous maintenance process, someone goofed and painted over the CG band, obscuring its identification. An assumption was made as to the correct CG

12. The Weapon Maintenance Plants

location on the weapon, but unfortunately, it was incorrect by several inches. As the primary lifting band was slowly lowered and the secondary band raised the weapon, its nose started to slowly tip down. Realizing the weapon was tipping, an officer and a Weapons Specialist standing close by grabbed the rear harness attempting to keep the weapon level. Three or four additional people joined in and slowly the weapon stopped moving and returned to the original position. A potential catastrophic nuclear accident was averted. Everyone in the plant was in a panic; how could someone act so irresponsibly as to paint the CG band? Such a thing should never happen. The Weapons Specialist received a commendation for his quick response and said, "I did notice that the four-star star general was gone when we got the MK 17 secured, and I never saw the general again." The government official didn't say a word, but everyone knew that something was sure to hit the fan. Several people were interviewed the following week but apparently no heads rolled. However, shortly thereafter a new Standard Operating Procedure (SOP) was issued detailing the correct way to repaint a weapon. The new SOP specifically pointed out that the CG band was not to be painted.

In addition to functioning as a weapons maintenance plant, according to research information, one portal was also designed for use as a Presidential Emergency Facility (PEF) and an alternate military headquarters command post in the event of a national emergency. Although not always the case, a PEF is often constructed as a hardened site or a site hardened to withstand a nuclear blast, and Manzano certainly qualified in that perspective.[9] The Manzano PEF was retained until the thermonuclear bomb was introduced, at which time it was no longer regarded a survival site. However, the timeline concerning the use of a PEF at Manzano WSA is somewhat problematic. In 1953, Site R, the Alternate Joint Communications Center, and a Department of Defense emergency relocation site at Mount Weather became operational, and the Manzano PEF function no longer existed. A mystery exists concerning what happened to its replacement. No documentation has surfaced suggesting the replacement for the Manzano PEF in the western United States. According to information I received from a Manzano caption and security OIC, there were a lot of interesting things at this location, including living quarters, a dining hall, a dispensary, and a morgue. There was always water running in the drains almost year-round. This tunnel

Part IV—The Restricted "Q" Area

retained its original function until the introduction of the thermonuclear weapon, at which time it was no longer regarded as a survivable site and was converted back into its original storage purpose.

Manzano base functioned for over 40 years as a maintenance and storage site for a variety of nuclear weapons and other materials. After the 1971 base merge with Kirtland, until the base closed in 1992, the routine service and maintenance work originally performed on weapons at the four plants was consolidated into Plants III and IV. These plants remained in use until the maintenance work was transferred to the new Kirtland weapons storage facility. During this time, Plant I was utilized as a communications center for the security police, and Sandia Laboratories continued to use the underground plant for testing and storage. Plant II was used as storage space for various nuclear components and other equipment.

13

The Birdcage for Pit Storage

The earliest atomic weapons were considered fission bombs, which used a sub-critical mass of radioactive material, either uranium or plutonium or a mixture of both, depending on the weapon type, as an explosion charge to initiate a nuclear blast. This radioactive material was contained in a sphere called a "capsule" or "pit," which ranged in size between a grapefruit and a small bowling ball, and weighed 11 to 13 pounds. The pit, named after the hard core found in fruits such as peaches and apricots, was the core of the implosion. To successfully initiate fission, the pit was not only compressed but additional neutrons were introduced to start the reaction by inserting an initiator into the center of the pit. These first nuclear weapon removable pits were loaded on an aircraft simultaneously with the weapon casing and installed into the bomb shortly before the bomb's deployment. To arm the bomb, a crewman would lower himself down into the bomb bay, with only

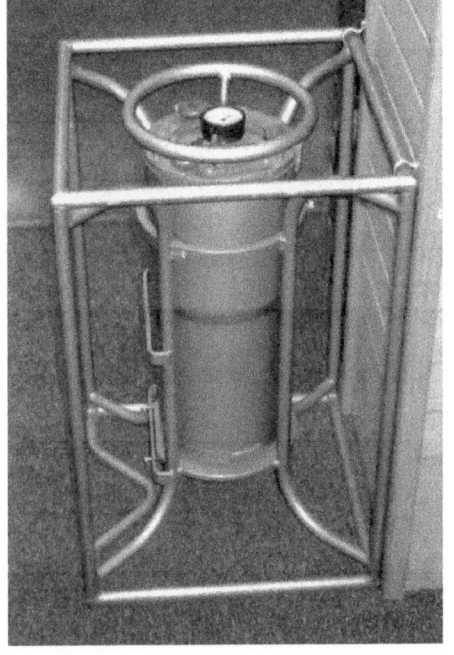

The birdcage special container (Ellsworth Air Force Base and RCG&A).

Part IV—The Restricted "Q" Area

the aluminum aircraft covering between him and the ground some 10,000 feet below, open the bomb trapdoor, push the pit into the bomb, and close up the bomb. The entire process took about 30 minutes.

Because of their volatility, pits required a storage structure separate from the weapon casing. While in storage the pits required regular maintenance because the spherical mass of plutonium would oxidize, requiring cleaning, and because the early initiators used polonium and beryllium. The polonium isotope, Pu 210, had a half-life of only 138 days, and each pit required periodic maintenance so that the initiator could be replaced. This process required the disassembly of the weapon pit to remove the initiator, which was at the center of the pit. Levitated pits were tested in 1948 with the Fat Man, MK 4, plutonium core style bomb. Over the years, several different type pits were developed, including a hollow pit, a solid-core Christy pit, composite cores and uranium pits, sealed pits, and linear implosion pits, each type changing and improving the efficiency of the implosion characteristics of a bomb.[1]

These removable pits, referred to as an "open pit," were housed in a special container called a "birdcage." The photograph at the beginning of this chapter is a M102 bird cage, the first pressurized safekeeping container, which ensured storage of the pit in a criticality-safe manner. The birdcages were stored in either type A or A-2 structures, as discussed in Chapter Eleven. Special security measures were incorporated into the construction of the storage structures at Plant I, which included heavy steel vault doors with two combination locks, and no single person knew both combinations.

After maintenance was complete, the pit/capsule was placed back within the birdcage, the lid secured with a lead seal, the container pressurized with inert gas, and returned to a storage structure. Needless to say, the element of danger around the pits in the cages was significant. The four arms of the specially designed container kept the cages adequately separated, because keeping them too close together could increase the risk of emitting an increased level of radiation. The top of the cage had a combination lock to provide access to the pit housed within it, ensuring limited access.

As a young airman waiting to attend technical school, a nuclear weapons specialist candidate said he was volunteered to guard six

13. The Birdcage for Pit Storage

birdcages being transported from San Francisco to Iwo Jima, Japan, and then return with six different cages. He said, "When I found out what they were, it made me uncomfortable to be that close to them. I always tried to maintain a safe distance between me and them."

A weapons technician at Manzano recalled a conversation he had in 1954 with a civilian from the Sandia Corp.: "He told me that in 1945 the scientists at Los Alamos were not too sure of the long-term effects of gamma radiation. They knew it was dangerous but did not know what level of intensity was dangerous." He described a demonstration called "Tickling the Tiger's Tail" or "Tickling the Tail of the Dragon," in which enriched plutonium was held between two hemispheres of beryllium, separated by the blade of a screwdriver. He explained that "when the screwdriver blade was rotated, the radiation increased exponentially, and the blue glow of ionized air was visible. The person holding the screwdriver kept an arm's length away and only conducted the demonstration for a brief time. One day in 1946, during a demonstration, the screwdriver slipped out of the hands of Louis Alexander Slotin, a Canadian physicist and chemist from the Manhattan Project." The two hemispheres came together, causing the core to momentarily go critical before Slotin flung the upper hemisphere away. "A huge flux of gamma rays was emitted. People watching the demonstration were amazed at the amount of energy produced by the gamma rays but were far enough away from the explosion that it caused them no harm. Unfortunately, Mr. Slotin became sick a week later, lost all his hair, developed a very low white cell blood account, and died nine days after the accident. The Sandia Corp. civilian telling the story said the experiment was never repeated."

Because uranium and plutonium are very susceptible to corrosion, these second-generation pits/capsules, brought into the inventory as of late 1954, still required periodic disassembly to verify the integrity of the fissile materials. Many pit designs were standardized with the capability of being shared between different weapons. Many pits are reusable, and the sealed pits extracted from disassembled weapons are normally placed in stock for future use. With the low aging rates of the plutonium-gallium alloy, the shelf life of pits can be more than a century. The oldest pits in the United States arsenal are still less than 50 years old. The on-going process to miniaturize the pit prompted design changes, whereby the pit could be inserted in the factory during the weapon assembly process. As of 1962, open pits/capsules were completely phased out, and AEC maintenance activities with nuclear materials ceased.

The Rocky Flats Plant, located 16 miles from Denver, Colorado, was a manufacturing complex that produced replacement pits for the U.S. nuclear stockpile. In 1989, the FBI shut down the plant because of environmental violations, and the plant was closed in 1992 at the instruction of President George H.W. Bush. The pit production process was transferred to the Los Alamos National Laboratory in 1997, and pit production in the United States ended in 2011.[2]

The United States has not produced a new nuclear weapon since 1991; however, to maintain a ready to use arsenal, existing warheads undergo upgrades on a regular basis to extend their active status. The United States currently has some 15,000 pits stored at a facility in Texas. The increased national security concerns have changed the concept and attitude of nuclear capability. A 2018 news article indicated that the U.S. National Nuclear Security Administration (NNSA) had requested the resumption of plutonium pit production and a significant increase in the levels of "plutonium equivalent" from 38.6 grams to 400 grams for material stored at a New Mexico nuclear facility.[3] The NNSA intent was to expand its production at the Los Alamos National Laboratory to approximately 30 pits per year and 50 pits per year at the Savannah River Site in South Carolina.[4] In June 2019, the NNSA published a notice of intent in the Federal Register to complete environmental reviews on its request to expand plutonium pit production for new and refurbished nuclear weapons. If this request is approved, the Los Alamos National Laboratory would be instrumental in the increased production.

Part V
Base Security

14

DoD Nuclear Weapon Storage Area Security Program

When the National Security Act of 1947 established the Department of Defense (DoD), it also created the U.S. Air Force as a separate branch of service. On January 1, 1948, General Order number one from USAF Headquarters designated those transferred aircraft security units and personnel as Air Police. Air Force Regulation (AFR) 355–4 issued on March 3, 1953, formally defined responsibilities for air base defense, and the Air Police was charged with responsibility beyond just protecting aircraft. As the weapons storage sites became active, a more defined nuclear weapon security program was required. The security program for a nuclear weapon storage site, such as Manzano, is a combination of human engagement and a systems-based, technological approach designed to work jointly to achieve the objective of preventing or defeating any overt and covert actions attempt perpetrated by an adversary. As specified in the DoD Nuclear Weapon Security Program, the base commander of a nuclear weapons storage site is charged with preventing unauthorized access, damage or sabotage, destruction, loss of control, capture or theft, and use of nuclear weapons, nuclear weapon systems, and all nuclear critical components.

As prescribed by the DoD Nuclear Weapon Security Program, the objectives of the security program are designed to:

- deny unauthorized access to nuclear weapons.
- prevent damage or sabotage to nuclear weapons.
- prevent loss of control of nuclear weapons.
- prevent an unauthorized nuclear detonation.
- prevent radiological contamination, to the extent possible.
- ensure weapons are available for use upon demand.

14. DoD Nuclear Weapon Storage Area Security Program

The DoD Directive 5201-41, Criteria and Standards for Safeguarding Atomic Weapons, issued December 8, 1962, is very specific in outlining the guarding of a storage site. This excerpt is extracted from the directive.

The guard force, when effectively utilized, is the most important single element in the security of an activity. Aids and adjuncts to armed guards for effecting adequate security are:

The Department of Defense seal.

Physical barriers and intrusion alarm devices.
Protective lighting.
Sentry dogs.
Circulation control systems.

Guards and custodians who protect atomic weapons will be armed and will use force, if necessary, in protecting weapons assigned to their custody.

Measures will be established to effect positive control over access into limited and exclusion areas and other locations as determined necessary by the respective commanders.

Patrols are appropriate for providing security coverage. In large areas, they should focus their activity on the specific area requiring protection and not principally on the perimeter of the entire site. Combined foot and motor patrols, or foot-sentry-dog patrols, combined with motor patrols normally provide satisfactory patrol activity. This does not preclude the use of one-man sentries or patrols, provided that reports are made at appropriate intervals to a central guard station. During hours of darkness and reduced visibility, the effectiveness of types of patrols for area surveillance, based on the general case, are rated in the following order:

a. Foot sentry-dog team.
b. Sentry.
c. Motorized patrol.

Local considerations will determine the particular type of patrol utilized.

The manning factor per guard post, or position, will be based on the policy of the service furnishing the personnel.

Emergency forces will be pre-designated and will be organized, manned,

Part V—Base Security

and equipped on the basis of the local situation and security interests involved. These forces, as a minimum, will consist of the following, subject however to any overriding requirements of the particular security interests involved:

    a. The Sabotage Alert Team—Two or more persons capable of responding within five minutes.

    b. The Backup Alert Force—Those personnel necessary to reinforce the Sabotage Alert Team within ten minutes.

    c. The Reserve Force—Those personnel necessary to support the on-duty security force within one hour.

These directives were uniformly implemented for each nuclear weapons storage site across the United States and modified as needed to ensure our nuclear weapons stockpile is protected even today.

15

Security Squadrons Responsible for Manzano

Security at Manzano WSA involved several different units from the time construction began through its closing. The security unit name changed several times during this time period, but the objective always remained the same: secure the installation and defend and protect personnel, equipment, and resources from hostile forces.

When the construction of phase I started, the district engineer was assigned the responsibility of security, and the Army 8455th Military Police Company was the first military group to provide security as the U.S. Corp of Engineers constructed the WSA. The U.S. Military Police Corps traces its lineage and history back to the American Revolution (1775–1783) when General George Washington requested that the staff position of provost marshal be created to deal with military disciplinary problems. On May 20, 1778, Congress established the Provost Corps, which Gen. Washington referred to as the "Maréchaussée Corps," a designation originally created by England's King William I to replace the French Gendarmerie. Over time, the word gendarmerie had developed a somewhat negative connotation, so King William called the new force The Corps de Maréchaussée, which is just an alternate, and more acceptable, French word for gendarmerie. This special unit was charged with protecting the encampment and maintaining order. When the army was camped, the Maréchaussée patrolled the area surrounding the camp, checking personnel passes and arresting spies, rioters, and drunkards. They enforced the high discipline standards set for the Continental Army soldiers. They were noted for carrying a pair of flintlock pistols on their saddle and consequently, the crossed flintlock pistols insignia continues to represent the Military

Part V—Base Security

Left: **Military Police shield.** *Right:* **Air Police shield.**

Police units. Capt. Bartholomew Von Heer, a German-speaking officer from Pennsylvania, was appointed as the first commander of the U.S. Maréchaussée on June 1, 1778. The United States continued to develop and use these Maréchaussée police units in the normal course of military business of providing security for the military base personnel and assets.[1]

World War I required a group of specially-trained soldiers to handle the massive numbers of prisoners of war and control the movement of troops and supplies in the zones of operation. To fulfill that need, Congress allowed for the permanent organization of Army Police units in the amendment to the National Defense Act in 1920. With the United States involved in World War II, and the impending activation of the Manhattan Project, time was of the essence to set up a more functional security program. After consideration and debate, in February 1942 the United States decided to adopt the British air defense philosophy, which was primarily designed to defend Army bases against local ground attacks. In June 1942, Gen. George C. Marshall, Army Chief of Staff, issued an order, which formed the Army Air Force (AAF) air base security battalions and referred to

15. Security Squadrons Responsible for Manzano

its members as Military Police (MP). On March 29, 1943, the commander of the AAF, Gen. Henry H. "Hap" Arnold, established three separate MP groups: The "Guard Squadrons" provided law enforcement and security for bases within the United States; the "Military Police Companies" had responsibilities within the aviation groups; and the "Air Base Security Battalions" were to be the ground combat force of the AAF.[2]

After the U.S. Air Force was created in 1947, the air provost marshal position was established, and on January 2, 1948, the Military Police name was changed to the Air Police. In total, 22 MP Companies were identified as Air Police Squadrons with this change. The name Air Police remained in use until their assignments in Vietnam became more of a combat infantry-type role than the role of police. To more accurately reflect the changed security and combat aspect of their mission, the Air Police was re-designated the Security Police in October 1966. In January 1971, the Security Police career field was split into two separate functions: Law Enforcement Specialist and Security Specialist. Subsequently, the Air Force decided to reevaluate how the Security Police was organized, and they came to the realization it was ineffective to have only a few members specialized in the security function when many more were needed. Therefore, on October 31, 1997, the Security Police became the Security Forces, with all individual specialties merged into one Security Forces specialist AFSC. The Security Forces brought back the old concept, which transformed it into a combat type force once again.

Over time, this group was transformed from just a guard unit into an elite force, recognized throughout the Air Force for its professionalism and effectiveness. Members initially wore a brassard as a symbol of legal authority, identifying the wearer as an air policeman. In 1957, the brassard was replaced with an Air Police shield, which was worn while on duty. As further recognition, in 1957, Gen. LeMay personally chose a dark blue beret for the Strategic Air Command's Elite Guard. That change resulted in such a dramatic positive effect on the morale of security forces that several months later, the USAF uniform board approved replacing the white service cap with the blue beret for all AF/SP units; it was officially being worn worldwide in 1976. As an added symbol of professionalism of the members of this distinctive and highly recognized group, the Security Forces Creed was adopted.

Part V—Base Security

> I am a security policeman. I hold allegiance to my country, devotion to duty and personal integrity above all. I will wear my badge of authority with dignity and restraint, and will promote by example high standards of conduct, appearance, courtesy, and performance. I seek no favor because of my position. I preform my duties in a firm, courteous and impartial manner, irrespective of a person's color, race, religion, national origin or sex. I strive to merit the respect of my fellow Airmen and all with whom I come in contact.

During the 42 years of active service, security for Manzano Base was provided by several different groups as the oversight of Manzano changed. Some of the information relating to security responsibility for Manzano was obtained from an unpublished history of Manzano by an A1C in the 1608th Security Police Squadron, provided by the Kirtland AFB historian.[3] As best I can ascertain, the list below reflects the squadrons that fulfilled that responsibility.

Army's Manhattan District Military Police (1947–1952)

After the close of the Army-managed Manhattan Project at the end of World War II, the DoD relocated that project to Sandia Base for the continuation of atomic weapons research, design, development, and testing, and, simultaneously, Site Able was developed as the first weapons storage site. According to my research, the Army's 8455th Manhattan District Military Police provided security for the Army's 8460th Special Weapons Group during the construction process and for two years after the site became operational on April 4, 1950. A 2010 Manzano history document also states that the U.S. Army's 8455th Military Police Company was

U.S. Army Military Police Company (Fred the Oyster, Wikipedia).

15. Security Squadrons Responsible for Manzano

responsible for security. This MP company was originally assigned to Site Baker at Killeen Texas, until October 19, 1948, when it was reassigned to Sandia Base.[4]

1094th Air Police Squadron (1952–1971)

In January 1952, six Air Police flights from the Killeen Weapons Storage Site consisting of 56 airmen arrived at Site Able to begin work in preparation for the forthcoming base transfer. The Air Force 1094th Special Reporting Group was created in 1950, which would become the 1094th Aviation Depot Group in 1955, with three individual operating subsidiary units: the 1094th Aviation Depot Squadron, 1094th Support Squadron, and 1094th Air Police Squadron.

In late 1951, the entire 1094th Special Reporting Squadron from Killeen Weapons Storage Site was transferred to Site Able in New Mexico. The 1094th Air Police Squadron (APS) replaced the Manhattan District Military Police and performed the same duties as they did at Killeen. The transfer was complete on February 25, 1952, when Site Able was transferred to the Air Force, renamed Manzano Base, and managed by the 3098th Aviation Depot Squadron, reporting directly to Field Command, Armed Forces Special Weapons Project.

1094th Air Police Squadron patch (author's collection).

The 1094th APS remained active until October 27, 1964, when it was assimilated into the 1094th Support Squadron, and continued in place until July 1, 1971, when Sandia and Manzano bases merged with Kirtland AFB.

Part V—Base Security

4900th Security Police Squadron (1971–1977)

The Air Force Special Weapons Command (SWC) was established on December 1, 1949, as the primary source for scientific and technical information on special weapons development. It was a Major Command of the Air Force, equal to the Air Defense Command, Strategic Air Command, and Tactical Air Command. Shortly after being established, the SWC re-designated several units under the USAF Field Office of Atomic Energy, with no change in station. As best I can determine, on December 1, 1949, the SWC re-designated Kirtland's 2758th Experimental Wing as the 4901st Special Weapons Wing and then re-designated it the 4901st Support Wing–Atomic on July 1, 1951. The 4901st was subsequently re-designated 4900th Air Base Group (ABG), in 1952.

The 4900th ABG included the 4900th Security Police Squadron (SPS) and, according to the base consolidation plan, the 1094th Air Police Squadron was consolidated under the 4900th SPS in the merge on July 1, 1971, and became responsible for Manzano security. A former airman made the statement: "I was stationed at Kirtland with the 4900th SPS (July 73–Oct 74) and assigned duty inside the fences at Manzano. The weapons base was closed but opened to accommodate a project called Operation Transition, teaching skills to AF personnel who were separating in six months. They opened the chow hall during this time, and the food was fantastic. Our Communications Center was deep in one of the tunnels. Manzano was a great assignment for a Security Specialist. Not counting rivets on a B-52." The 4900th functioned as a Wing through July 1, 1977, when it was replaced with the 1606th Air Base Wing.

1606/1608th Security Police Squadron (1977–1989)

Kirtland's command changed again on July 1, 1977, when the Military Airlift Command took control, inactivating the 4900th Air Base Wing and replacing it with the Air Force Systems Command 1606th Air Base Wing, acquiring responsibility for Manzano base security. A former AF major and OIC of Manzano security said, "In 1978, the 1606th was separated into two units: the 1606th

15. Security Squadrons Responsible for Manzano

Security Police Squadron—Law Enforcement and Administration and 1608th Security Police Squadron for Manzano. We were always short on personnel for the mountain, so we would pull 1606 guys to make sure we manned all positions. The incoming 1st Lt. Flight Commanders had to be reminded that Law Enforcement was fun, but Manzano could be their downfall, and most of them got it right. We were the only special weapons unit in the Military Airlift Command." On September 1, 1979, Air Force officials established the Air Force Office of Security Police at Kirtland Air Force Base.

1606/1608th Security Police-Squadron patch (Kirtland AFB).

377th Security Forces Group (1989–1992)

On January 1, 1993, the combat-decorated 377th Air Base Wing was re-activated and became the new host unit of Kirtland Air Force Base. The 377th Security Forces Group and 377th Weapons Systems Security Squadron were activated in 2011, and the 377th Security Police assumed security responsibility. A former 377th airman stated, "I

377th Security Forces Group patch (USAF, Kirtland AFB).

worked on the mountain from 1989 to 1992, and was a member on one of the convoy teams that moved the contents of the mountains into the Kirtland Underground Munitions Maintenance and Storage complex." Another member of the 377th SPS told me he was assigned to Manzano from January 1992 until it closed in September 1992.

Sandia National Laboratories (1992–Present)

Sandia National Laboratories assumed responsibility for security after the base official closed and continues to provide security for Manzano security gates, patrols, electronics, and fences. The 377th Security Forces at Kirtland has concurrent jurisdiction and is available to assist Sandia if needed.

16

The Perimeter Fences

Most military installations are protected with some type of fencing to prevent unauthorized entrance. In a nuclear weapons storage site, fencing is of utmost importance because it's the first line of defense to deter and deny entrance. The nuclear material housed within the WSS requires the greatest security consideration to increase the difficulty of intrusion. Physical barriers, lighting, and intrusion alarms are specifically addressed in the Criteria and Standards for Safeguarding Atomic Weapons, DoD Directive 5201-41, issued December 8, 1962. The excerpt below is from that directive.

1. Physical barriers will clearly delineate the zone of protection of security areas and provide a positive means of denying or impeding access thereto. A minimum of one line of physical barriers will be established to protect permanent security areas provided for the safeguarding of atomic weapons. Where permanent physical barriers are considered impractical because of the temporary nature of storage or for other reasons, the absence of the perimeter barrier will be compensated for by additional guard posts, patrols, sentry-dog patrols, or other security measures.

2. Security lighting will be provided for all areas in such a manner as to discourage, and facilitate the detection of, attempts of unauthorized entry into established security areas or the structures in which atomic weapons are stored. Where such lighting provisions are impractical, their absence will be compensated for by additional guard posts, patrols, sentry-dog patrols, or other security measures.

3. Intrusion alarm systems provided for security protection should be simple in design with operational objectives of dependability and ruggedness. The paramount purpose of such alarms will be to provide useful and practicable assistance to the guard force.

The 11-mile base perimeter was surrounded by three chain-link fence lines about 10 feet apart, each approximately 10 to 12 feet high, with the middle fence electrified with an estimated 20,000 volts. For easy location identification, the mountain was subdivided into three

Part V—Base Security

The perimeter security fences (Norio Hayakawa).

areas designated Alpha, Charlie and Bravo, and further identified with section numbers for the fence. Some of the fence lines were equipped with ADT sensors and lighting, designed to trigger the alarm in the event of an attempted penetration. A perimeter road was located around the entire base, providing the security force easy and quick access to any section of fence.

The ADT sensors detected any attempt to penetrate the boundary of the weapon storage site and were paired with a perimeter light sensor system. An A1C Weapons Specialist, stationed there in 1956, said lights were originally installed around the entire perimeter fence, and if any section incurred an attempted penetration, the lights around the entire perimeter illuminated. Any time an alarm activation occurred, it created base-wide panic and a full alert posture for the security team on duty. After several occurrences, the base commander suggested it would be more effective in locating the section of potential penetration if only that section of fence was illuminated. The change was made, and it worked very effectively, preventing any future disruption of the entire base.

16. The Perimeter Fences

Activation alarms did, however, create disruptions for the security flight working the mountain. Occasionally a small animal would get caught between the fences and couldn't find its way out. If by chance the animal came in contact with the electrified fence, it would trigger the alarm for that section—and an immediate reaction by the security response team. A member of the 4900th APS described a typical patrol scenario responding to a fence alarm this way: "CSC (Central Security Control) to Alpha 3. We have a fence alarm on section 105, respond ASAP. Alpha 3 responds, 10–4 in route. In a couple of minutes Alpha 3 is on the scene and radios back to CSC, we are on location, and it's just another smoking rabbit. CSC replies, 10–4 Alpha 3, stand by while he burns off and we reset the fence alarm. Alpha 3 replies, 10–4." With the situation resolved, everything returns to the normal routine.

Any intrusion alarm, whether fence, plant or structure, always creates anxiety. A 1992 377th SPS TSgt Supervisor tells of one alarm occurrence this way: "The perimeter fence activated an alarm status in Close Boundary Patrol India 3's area one night, and India 3 responded. In a couple of minutes, they came over the radio to India 4, the supervising patrol: 'India 4! INDIA 4! RESPOND ASAP!' So, we hauled ass over there. When we arrived, we saw something totally engulfed in flame on the inside the electric fence, which they told us later that it was a bobcat." Apparently, that was India 3 patrol team's first encounter with this type of situation, but I suspect not the last.

With the numerous security measures in place around the mountain, experts were convinced that the possibility of unauthorized entry onto the base was virtually non-existent, and that was true from 1947 until 1971. A captain and former director of security at Manzano tells me that changed on January 25, 1971, when two Mexican farm laborers penetrated all fences, gaining entry onto the base. As programmed, the fence alarm was set off, the lights came on, a 15-member security team charged to be on location in five minutes was dispatched, and the two men were apprehended. When questioned, they said they were looking for food and work and thought the area was the ranch of a rich person.

Needless to say, the base security group received immense criticism from the military, newspapers, and local residents. How these men got onto the base was never publicly disclosed, but the director of security told me that the base Civil Engineering Group, for an unknown reason, had decreased the fence power without advising other base agencies. I suspect those members of the Civil Engineering Group responsible for the breach, received more than criticism. This may have been the only security breach in the 42 active years of Manzano, and if that is true, that is a pretty good record.

With all the secrecy surrounding the base, being able to breach security and sneak on the base was challenging to some people. In fact, an A1C tells me that in 1956 a reporter for the *Albuquerque Journal* boasted that he could do just that without getting caught. The Air Police caught wind of this boast and waited. Someone set up a money pool for the AP who caught or shot him. The reporter was unable to get past the perimeter road and luckily didn't get shot. So collapsed his boasting.

The three fences alone should produce a feeling of trepidation for anyone and should have been quite a discouragement to attempt entry onto base. Seeing the posted no trespassing signs and not knowing the nomenclature of the fences, a reasonable person should have anticipated the possibility that at least one could be electrified. However, the best efforts to deter were not always successful. In May 1972, two Albuquerque teenagers tried to sneak onto the base. Ignoring the posted warning signs, they successfully penetrated the first fence, but one teen touched the second fence and was electrocuted by a reported 20,000 volt charge.[1]

17

Storage Structure Security System

Protecting the nuclear weapon while in storage is a number one priority. Tunneling into the mountains provided a significant amount of natural protection, and the free-standing structures were covered by more than 30 feet of soil to provide additional protection. Security team members could provide substantial protection for any action that was initiated on the ground but protecting a weapon from aircraft flying above was a greater concern. This perception did not necessarily anticipate an intentional bombing of the structure, but aircraft carrying conventional and nuclear weapons were flying over the mountains on a regular basis. The question was, if a plane carrying a conventional 2,000-pound bomb crashed into—or close by—a structure, would the nuclear weapon inside the structure sustain any damage? An analysis was conducted and the conclusion reached was that the tunnels were safe because of their depth into the mountain, and because of the 30 feet of earth covering the free-standing structures, no damage was probable. This analysis proved correct with the crash of a B-29 in 1950, referenced in Chapter Twenty-one.

As required by the DoD Directive 5201-41, each structure, plant, and building involving nuclear weapon activity was equipped with an ADT alarm system, monitored by an individual in a portal on the west side of the mountain, next to the Central Security Control (CSC). In 1964, the alarm system was supervised by civilian ADT operators, and some years later that function was turned over to the Security Police, and the alarm maintenance was performed by Air Force personnel or civilian contractors. In the event the alarm was set off, a security force team was dispatched to investigate. A 377th Security Force member told me that in 1992 the objective was to have 15 armed team members respond to an alarm within

Part V—Base Security

five minutes (15/5). Because the storage area was so large, there were multiple 15/5 response teams. These ADT alarms were not sensitive, so it took a fair amount of effort to set them off, like someone kicking one at 0300 hours to give the area patrol team something to do.

A captain and assistant chief of Security Police told this story: "After the 1971 merger, something or someone was routinely setting off storage structure alarms, with no clue as to what or whom it could possibly be. At that time, Sandia National Laboratories housed a few bush apes in cages for experimentation purposes, and unfortunately a couple of them escaped. The rumor was that the apes made it to the mountain and were setting off the alarms. But how they could have gotten into the Q Area undetected? The answer somehow escaped the theorists. In an attempt to prove—or disprove—the ape rumor, one weekend I formed a human chain of our troops, and we walked up and over the mountain, inside the Q Area. We didn't find an ape habitat but found an old mining shaft. Unfortunately, no one would venture down into it. So, that's where the bush apes live, right? Despite the rumors, I never doubted the alarms were being surreptitiously set off by bored SPs." Eventually, the frequency of the alarms subsided, so if it had been the apes, I assume these primates found more exciting things to do.

By DoD directive, any location containing nuclear weapons must be opened only when necessary for operations, system testing, required maintenance, inventory, weapon movement, inspections and, in some instances, training. When someone needed to enter a structure they contacted the Manzano CSC in advance, gave the necessary authorization information, and, in some cases, provided a passcode, which changed daily. A security team was dispatched to the structure, to remain there until it was closed and once again secure.

To ensure uniform procedures in securing nuclear weapons, the Air Force developed a Nuclear Surety Tamper Control and Detection Program. Part of this program established the procedures for sealing by:

- imposing restrictions as to when, and by whom, seals can be applied or removed;
- implementing controls for the issue, receipt, storage, and

17. Storage Structure Security System

disposal of tamper detection indicators-controlled dies, and self-locking, non-reversible seals; and
- establishing mandatory requirements to ensure only two-person teams install seals and verify they remain intact.

Additionally, the program mandated conducting periodic inspections of seals on nuclear weapon-loaded aircraft, missile systems, and certified critical components in storage or transport.[1]

Each time a Manzano structure was entered and then closed, the steel door was shut and locked and the alarm was reset. A metal strip seal was secured in place on the door and the serial number on the seal was recorded in a log retained at CSC. Sealing is the method used to indicate any attempt to tamper with a structure containing a weapon. A crimping tool is used to apply to the seal, and through its unique design or markings, minimizes the possibility of counterfeiting, substituting, removing or reinstalling a seal.

During my years at the base, 1964 through 1966, at the beginning of each patrol shift, the first order of business was to check each structure to ensure the lock was secure, see the seal was in place, and verify the seal number to the list we were provided. If either the lock or seal appeared to have been tampered with, we immediately notified the flight commander, secured the area, and stayed at the structure until the situation was resolved. A Security Police team member assigned to Manzano in 1992 said, "When I was there, the structures had seals and were on a two-hour check schedule by the Security Patrol Team responsible for the structures."

18

Central Security Control and ADT Monitoring

Once the perimeter security had been installed and the security system connected, a designated control location needed to be established and a monitoring process activated. For Manzano, this control location was in Portal A, tunneled deep into the mountain. Referred to as the Central Security Control center (CSC), it housed the ADT control room and was the hub to ensure total security for the WSS.

During the day shift, there was a lot of activity in the "Q" area requiring additional security precautions. Several of the 121 structures were being opened and closed, and weapons were relocated from plants to structures or loaded on trucks to be convoyed off base. Therefore, the need for a CSC was much greater. Such activities did not usually occur on the swing (1600 to 2400 hours) or midnight (2400 to 0800 hours) shifts, so the CSC security operations' responsibility was closed at the end of the day shift and transferred from Portal A to the shift NCOIC in the guard house, just inside the Q Area.

Just down the hall from CSC was the ADT operations room with a monitoring system manned by two or three duty flight security personnel and, in 1966, under the oversight of an ADT civilian supervisor. It operated 24/7/365. A former AP said the procedure, in 1955, was to station one security guard at the portal entrance and one guard inside the tunnel at the entrance to the maintenance plant, to check the badge of every person entering. The portal doors remained open during normal daytime working hours and closed all other times.

Ensuring security while keeping track of the work activity within the Q Area was a challenge to say the least. To aid in this monitoring

18. Central Security Control and ADT Monitoring

process, a large map of the entire Q Area, referred to as the ADT Board, was mounted on the wall in front of the ADT Operators (shown on Appendix B). The board shows every structure, plant, storage building, and portal on the mountain, and the alarm for each of these was connected to the ADT board. A small status box is mounted on the board at each structure, plant, portal and building to indicate the on-going security status. The status box contains three lights. A green light indicates the structure is secure. If the structure, plant, portal, or storage facility was to be opened for any purpose, a pre-set opening process was followed, and an amber light would display on the board, indicating it was open but under guard. Once the doors were closed and the structure was secure again, the green light would re-illuminate. Any potential security breach of the fence, structure, plant or portal would set off an alarm, and a red light on the board would blink, prompting a responsive action by security patrols and a 15/5 security team. The board also showed the perimeter fence divided into sections, and the hot fence indicated with a red stripe. Each section was equipped with an alarm connected to the ADT board.

CSC entrance at Portal "A" (Kirtland AFB and RCG&A).

A 1094th A1C AP, who worked in the ADT Operations during 1953, stated, "Working in ADT operations was a nice relief from the boredom of staffing the Main Gate, the Q Gate, the standby posts, or riding patrol inspecting structures and plants. We were allowed to read and study while on duty during the swing and midnight shifts, and on weekends. Otherwise, we remained alert at our duty station." Normally, working in CSC/ADT was quiet and uneventful. However, there were those occasions when an alarm went off, and all hell broke loose. The ADT board red light start to blink, the

Part V—Base Security

anxiety level intensified, a 15/5 security team was dispatched, radio chatter increased, and apprehension prevailed until the alarm was investigated, resolved, and reset. The A1C said, "Once in a while, one of the patrol team members would kick the door of a structure just to see what kind of reaction they could get from CSC. On occasion, the sound was loud enough to set off alarms at several other structures simultaneously, and from the ADT's monitoring perspective, it would look like a jet plane just did a low-level fly over, or a lightning strike had rattled several structure sensors."

The ADT operator tells me, "In 1998, 50 former air policemen had the opportunity to revisit the old CSC and ADT Operations room. I was surprised that the ADT Board was in place, and still looked pretty good, although it was covered with dust. Seeing it again brought back many old memories of situations, events, and people with whom I worked. It was a great trip down memory lane."

The A1C also said, "While working in the CSC room one midnight shift, we were startled by what sounded like a terrific explosion. We rushed out into the corridors to see what had exploded only to find the AP, guarding the inside of Portal A, had gotten so bored with doing nothing that he fired his 45 Cal weapon at the portal door. The explosion we heard was the sound of the shot reverberating off the hard tunnel wall surfaces, but we were horror-struck for a few minutes."

The CSC also contained a power generator backup for the electrical system. A major with the 1608th SPS told me: "Under a lend-lease program, marine electric generators were on a U.S. ship destined for Murmansk, Russia, probably for use on a Russian ship. Realizing the end was nearing for the Third Reich, the generators were returned to the United States, transported to Manzano, and installed in Portal A as a backup in case there was a failure with commercial power. These generators were capable of producing sufficient electricity to support the electric perimeter fence, the lights on all structures, the maintenance plants, and CSC. There was just one small problem with using the generators. Several of the operating instruction manuals were printed in Russian. Needless to say, a linguist was on stand-by, and CSC always had two electricians from Civil Engineering on duty to bring the generators on line, synchronize the power, and carry the load." A 1094th AP was working

18. Central Security Control and ADT Monitoring

CSC in 1959 when the base lost power and said, "I watched as a civil engineer and a helper started up and ran the giant gas or diesel engines. It had pistons larger than basketballs and noisy as a freight train." These huge generators were replaced in the 1978 security upgrade.

19

Patrolling the "Q" Area

In previous chapters, we discussed the security protocols in place at Manzano, including the personnel background investigation, access restrictions, perimeter fencing, security systems, and monitoring capabilities for the plants and structures, which were tested on a regular basis. In addition, the 24/7/365 security patrol was a critical function in the protection of the nuclear weapons storage site, and its importance was never taken lightly. As noted in Chapter Fourteen, the 1962 DoD Directive 5201-41 set the standards for safeguarding atomic weapons, stating: "The guard force, when effectively utilized, is the most important single element in the security of an activity. Guards and custodians who protect atomic weapons will be armed *and will use force, if necessary*, in protecting weapons assigned to their custody." Once issued weapons, every security team member understood what he might be required to do.

Security guards were charged with the responsibility to prevent unauthorized access, damage or sabotage, unauthorized destruction, loss of control, capture or theft, and unauthorized use of nuclear weapons, nuclear weapon systems, and all nuclear critical components. Every patrol shift comprehended the gravity of the task they were undertaking for the next eight hours.

The 1094th Air Police Security Squadron was comprised of four to five flights, depending on the time period, with 25 to 30 people per flight. A junior officer, usually a first lieutenant, was assigned as a shift commander and usually stayed in the squadron commander's office unless called out on an incident. Each flight worked rotating day, swing, midnight and training/relief shifts, and off days were included in each duty cycle. In 1965, we were on a three-day rotation schedule. We were always subject to recall, even on our days off. A recall plan was established for each flight, with the goal of a one-hour response time, and this plan was tested on a regular basis. If you

19. Patrolling the "Q" Area

Typical security patrol vehicle (USAF Police Alumni Association).

failed to make the recall time without a good reason, the NCOIC was noted to say, you can give your soul to heaven because your ass is mine.

In addition to the security tests conducted by Manzano personnel, periodic exercises by outside security units were also orchestrated. In his book, *A Gun and Cherries in a Bucket of Blood*, Craig Casadei, an intelligence officer assigned to the 901st Military Intelligence Detachment at Sandia Base, talks about one exercise his team conducted at Manzano. The exercise involved base penetration to test security personnel's propensity to follow procedure rather than doing things haphazardly.

To paraphrase his story, Craig says the exercise was initiated in the early morning hours when off-duty personnel were sleeping or just getting home from a night out, and on-duty personnel were tired, bored, and sleepy, and all likely to be aggravated by the exercise. The security force team on duty was told there was a "Q" area penetration, and several transgressors were at large—in fact, a couple of intelligence agents had been covertly brought into

Part V—Base Security

the "Q" area for the exercise. Craig and a team member were in an unmarked car on the perimeter road when they were approached by trucks with flashing red lights. Security police jumped out of the truck, pointed M-14s at them, and demanded they exit the vehicle and lie face down on the ground. Craig said, "The security police were breathing heavy with anxiety, and we knew the safety was off on their M-14s. We complied without hesitation because to do otherwise could have gotten us shot." When asked what they were doing on the road, Craig replied they were lost, a response which did not go over well. Craig and his partner were apprehended and taken to the NCOIC at CSC. Craig says overall, the exercise was deemed a success, and security personnel performed as expected. Craig also says, "Those of us on the wrong end of the M-14s were glad they did."[1]

This is just a typical security exercise experienced at Manzano. As would be expected, these exercises were designed to keep our perception sharp, ensure timely response, and hone our action skills. The exercises had a way of getting the adrenalin pumping quickly.

Prior to assuming our patrol duty, we convened for a guard mount at the armory, just inside the Q Gate. We drew our weapons from the armory and assembled into formation to be inspected by the flight commander. Even though we seldom came in contact with anyone besides other flight members, we were expected to be clean shaven, have an acceptable haircut, and wear clean fatigues, pressed with an arm and leg crease, a non-stained fatigue cap, and polished boots. If we didn't, we were subject to disciplinary action. During guard mount, we received any news updates, special instructions, and patrol assignment, and then we proceeded to our patrol area to relieve those already on duty.

As we will discuss a bit later in this chapter, practical jokes were always being played, if for no other reason than sheer boredom. An A1C stationed there in 1959 recounted a story about an airman who climbed to the roof of the Air Police barracks one afternoon and proceeded to "moon" the flight assembling for guard mount. I suspect he felt the need to express his opinion about something or to someone. Once he was observed—and despite the best effort of the assembled flight members to maintain composure—they burst out laughing, disrupting the instructions being given to them. Needless to say, that activity did not go over well with the flight commander, but search

19. Patrolling the "Q" Area

as he might, the culprit was never identified. Perhaps "message delivered" is an appropriate conclusion to the incident.

Over the years, the number of people on each flight changed, probably because of the type of weapons stored there and the increase in threat level. In 1964, each flight was comprised of 25 to 30 people. However, during 1978–1981, the 1608th SPS, OIC of Manzano security told me that they had some 60 people on duty at any time, with 15 people deployed per sector. A 377th SPS from Kirtland assigned to Manzano in 1992, said in total, 80 posts were manned on every shift. Two-man, close boundary patrols patrolled in each sector around the mountain, while a six-person mobile fire team in a pickup and a stationary fire team mobilized with a Peacekeeper armored truck were on stand-by. A flight commander, area supervisors, and an administrative person in the armory completed the full complement of shift personnel. Weapons for these patrols consisted of an M1, M16, M-203 or a M-60, depending on the time period, and a 45-caliber sidearm. Arms were drawn from the armory at the beginning of each shift and returned when the shift was over. Security force members were charged not to let any concern, obstacle, or situation deter their actions to neutralize an adversary.

At some point in time, the mountain was divided into three sectors, Alpha, Bravo, and Charlie. Accordingly, the two-man patrol teams in each sector were sequentially designated as Alpha 1, Bravo 1, Charlie 1, etc. Each patrol team was assigned a specific area within the sector, and for eight hours they drove back and forth within their area, ensuring all structures, plants, and buildings remained secure. Each sector contained a small trailer, where we took a break. During my time at Manzano in 1964, we patrolled for one and a half hours with a half-hour break in the trailer, which was always welcome because we could finally smoke. In 1965 smoking was not permitted on patrol, so many of us tried to perfect the art of chewing tobacco. Red Man, Apple, Brown Mule, and Beech Nut were a few of the favorite brands. Learning to chew, I and several others experienced two basic challenges: first, remembering not to swallow, and second, spitting out the window with sufficient force to avoid getting any tobacco juice on the vehicle door. Never perfecting the second challenge, I cleaned many a vehicle door in my two years there. For some reason, the motor pool always wanted two clean vehicle doors.

The patrols monitored all activity within their area, checking

Part V—Base Security

the roadways, structures, buildings, and culverts on a regular basis during their shift. If anything was questionable, the patrols were authorized to stop anyone or any vehicle and challenge their validity. In 1964, when a vehicle approached us at night we would flash the red light on top of our vehicle. If the approaching vehicle was a fellow AP, they would respond by returning a red-light flash. If no red-light flash was returned, we pulled our vehicle across the road, exited the vehicle, retrieved our M1 from the rack, and proceed to stop the oncoming vehicle. It was a tradition that each new AP be indoctrinated to this process during a midnight shift. When the new AP rider was nodding off about 0300 hours, the seasoned AP driver would drive close to a downhill embankment on the rider's side of the vehicle, turn on the red light and yell, "Challenge, Challenge." When the new AP, still half asleep, exited the vehicle, down the hill he would slide. The embankment was never steep enough to cause injury, but it was a vivid memory the next day as he polished his boots to get the scuff marks off them.

A 1094th AP stationed at Manzano in 1958 said, "There was an explosive test site outside the base on the east side, which usually drew several Atomic Energy Commission (AEC), DoD and Air Force personnel. The AEC personnel felt they could go anywhere they wanted in the Q Area without question, and by turning on the red light on the top of their vehicle, they were automatically cleared. We used to enjoy challenging them and have them show us their IDs. They got aggravated but reluctantly complied with our request." It was a break from the boredom of riding patrol.

Testing a patrol's response time and security protocol was done on a periodic basis. A captain and operations officer of the KAFB SP Squadron told this story. "The Kirtland Base commander was permitted to take his vehicle into the WSA without being subjected to a search. I convinced him to let me hide in the trunk of his car one night, and let me out on the other side of the mountain. I set off a structure alarm, then buried myself in a pile of tumbleweeds close by, unfortunately to discover I am allergic to them. The security patrol teams responded within the accepted time, and the troops searched the area, some walking within a few feet of my location, but didn't see me. With the tumbleweed getting the best of me, I finally gave up and told them I had a bomb hidden in my jacket and if they

19. Patrolling the "Q" Area

didn't let me go, I'd blow them up. They responded correctly, and figuratively shot me full of holes."

Patrolling on the day shift was always active with weapons shuttled to and from the plants, being on site for the opening and closing of structures or participating in a security convoy escorting a weapon to Sandia or Kirtland. However, patrolling on the swing and midnight shifts was always a challenge. After the sun went down, the mountain was extremely dark, except for the lights on the patrol vehicle. Unless the flight commander or a flight sergeant came into your patrol area, you never saw anyone. An SP stationed there in 1987 described it this way, "Patrolling on swing and midnight shifts was boring and eerily quiet," and another SP said, "During the midnight shift, it was pitch black and very creepy."

After several hours riding around the mountain, sleep would overtake patrol teams and the temptation to pull into a secluded area and grab 40 winks was very tempting. A 1956 1094th AP said, "To ensure patrols did not exceed the 25 mph speed limit, and make their rounds as prescribed, a Sangamo Tachograph was installed in each patrol truck. Within any set time frame, these devices could measure and record on a paper disc loaded inside the clock the vehicle's speeds, time sitting still, and total mileage. However, someone discovered that the vehicle ignition key would open the clock housing, and the paper spool could be removed and re-installed at the end of the shift. Additionally, someone discovered that inserting a hot metal pin into the plastic cover at a specific location would prevent the clock from recording speeds in excess of 25 mph." At the end of the shift, these disks were removed from each vehicle and checked. So, what was the repercussion if caught tampering with the tachograph? The AP telling the story added, "Taking the truck away and making us walk patrol was not fun, and especially at night." I can only imagine that scenario.

Saying it was boring is an understatement. Crazy things were done on patrol to fill the many hours of boredom. For example, one 1094th AP told this story: "There was a dirt road between two of the mountain peaks we called a saddle road. It was dangerous, off-limits, and we were not supposed to walk up there, much less drive over the mountain on it. But beyond that, it required the patrol to leave their designated patrol area, a violation of UCMJ Article 86 (2), punishable by confinement for three months and forfeiture of two-thirds pay per

Part V—Base Security

month for three months. Those were two pretty good incentives not to leave our patrol area, however, driving over the saddle was kind of a rite of passage. Many of us did it, and of course, always hoping the flight commander didn't come around during the venture or be close enough to see the vehicle headlights."

You always had to be on guard while on the mountain because practical jokes were as regular as guard mount, and anyone was subject to be the target anytime. Here is a typical example. In 1965, the motor pool often had a difficult time keeping patrol vehicles ready for use, and frequently a vehicle which had just completed an eight-hour shift would be turned around and sent back up for another shift. As indicated in the Chapter Eleven, the first order of business on every shift was to check the lock and verify the seal number on each structure in the patrol area. The list of structure seal numbers was kept on a sheet of paper on a small clipboard, which we put in the glove box after we completed the seal check.

One night working the midnight shift, my patrol partner and I were assigned a vehicle which had been turned around from the prior swing shift (1600–2400 hours). After we had completed the structure checks at about 0130 hours, I opened the glove box door and a two-foot-long bull snake fell into my lap, scaring me half to death. My other half was scrambling to find the door handle. Since a bull snake is not poisonous or aggressive, I probably scared it as much as it scared me. I did locate the door handle and made a quick exit, inviting the snake to do the same. If it was not a bull snake, it could have been a large tarantula just as easily, since they were also used for the same practical joke. From that point on, I opened the glove box very slowly and carefully. That is a lasting memory to this day.

One of the most original practical jokes was told to me by a 377th Security Police team member patrolling the mountain in 1992. He said, "Someone with a gorilla mask was sneaking around on a midnight shift scaring the crap out of people. I, along with my partner, was hit while patrolling on India 6 in Bravo sector about 0300 hours one cold winter morning. The vehicle was warm, we were tired, struggling to stay awake as the low moan of the heater fan lulled us into a dozing state of mind. I had stopped the vehicle to make a U-turn, when out of the corner of my eye I saw something move. As I turned my head, I saw this guy standing at my driver's window with

19. Patrolling the "Q" Area

that mask on. Scared the hell out of me. I jumped so hard my head hit the ceiling of that '91 Blazer, knocking my beret into the floorboard. By the time I grabbed my M-16 from the rack and jumped out of the truck, the guy had disappeared. I shouted out, 'I'm gonna get you sucker!' We never found out who it was, but for several weeks, the Manzano Monster made appearances in the early morning hours."

As previously mentioned, on the swing and midnight shifts CSC was closed and Security Operations resided in the guard house just inside the Q Area. A 1094th A1C AP told me about another practical joke involving a snake: "The guard house just inside the Q Gate was the location where we took a break from Alpha Section patrolling. There were vending machines in the guard house, and we were allowed to doze while awaiting our return to patrol duty. One night one of my rogue friends, an A2C, brought a dead rattlesnake into the guard house, threw it on the floor and yelled, 'Snake, snake!' Twenty APs scrambled in all directions, knocking over tables, and spilling coffee and soft drinks as they fled. That was the same airman who shot the door in Portal A one night. He never made the rank of airman first class."

Even though practical jokes were pervasive, we performed our duty, and the base remained secure month after month, year after year.

20

Nuclear Weapon Convoy Duty

Providing adequate security for nuclear weapons and components was a necessity from the beginning. That protection process was relatively easy in a stationary environment such as a storage site; however, the challenge came when those weapons were transported to another location. The logistical movement of nuclear cargo between installations is one of the Air Force's highest priority tasks, requiring protection from mishaps and terrorist or subversive threats. Each component of the movement from the departure to the arrival is critical, including the nature of cargo being moved, the time of departure and the estimated time of arrival, the security requirements, and priority handling of ground transportation. To facilitate and oversee each movement, an on-scene officer-coordinator was assigned, with the ability to resolve difficulties and elevate problems to the appropriate level if needed. The DoD considered transportation security to be a weak link in the security process and struggled with just how to transport and maintain the security necessary to protect the weapons.

As previously discussed in Chapter Twelve, the weapons maintenance plants, nuclear weapons and pits were changed out periodically as part of a routine inspection and maintenance function. Therefore, nuclear weapons requiring maintenance were arriving at Sandia Base and Kirtland AFB on a frequent basis and replaced with ready to go weapons housed in the structures at the Manzano WSA. Anytime a weapon or a nuclear component was transported to or from the Manzano "Q" area to Kirtland or Sandia, a security escort was always required as prescribed by the DoD Directive 5201-41. The excerpt below is extracted from that directive.

20. *Nuclear Weapon Convoy Duty*

A nuclear weapon convoy (U.S. Air Force).

F. Transportation:

1. The primary objective of the security requirements set forth below is to provide adequate safeguards to atomic weapons in logistical movement. In order to ensure adequate safeguards, consideration will be given to these requirements when weapons are moved under tactical training conditions.

2. The number of guard escorts, the type of weapons provided, and the type of escort vehicles required, if any, will be determined by the appropriate commander, based upon the particular type and means of shipment. As a minimum, the following requirements are applicable to couriers or military guards of atomic weapons:

    a. Couriers and guards assigned to safeguard atomic weapons will be in sufficient number to provide adequate relief in order that fatigue will not diminish their effectiveness.

    b. Couriers and guards will be appropriately armed, qualified, and selected in accordance with the provisions of Section V, paragraph B.

    c. Couriers and guards will ensure that access to atomic weapons during loading, off-loading, and in transit, is controlled in accordance with paragraph D above.

Part V—Base Security

  d. Emergency plans and procedures will be formulated and made known in detail to all shipment security personnel and others concerned. Such plans will include adequate communications system, appropriate liaison with government and law enforcement agencies, and action to be taken in the event of accident, unusual delay in route, attempted, or actual removal or damage, of shipment, possible compromise of information relating thereto, or other incidents affecting the successful completion of the mission.

Over the years, different methods were used to transport weapons as indicated in the following stories from book contributors.

Transportation by Railroad

A 1094th Weapons Specialist at Manzano tells me that on a weekly basis during 1953, several birdcages, each containing a single pit or cylinder, were loaded into a truck and under heavy guard, escorted to a secure loading dock at the Albuquerque train station. The birdcages were loaded onto a special railroad car to be transported to another location. Unlike a nuclear weapon, a birdcage weighed less than 100 pounds and was loaded or unloaded into the railroad car by two people, making the use of a forklift unnecessary. In 1964, we continued to escort weapons from Manzano to the secure railhead on Sandia Base—not as frequently as in 1953 but several times a month. The railhead was a spur off the main rail line, surrounded by a nine-foot chain-link fence, with a gate at each end for ingress and egress. Our responsibility was to get the weapon safely to the railhead, and once there, another security unit took the responsibility for the weapon.

My research into nuclear weapons rail transportation indicates that, from the 1950s through the 1980s, the most secure and safe method to transport nuclear weapons or pit birdcages from one location to another was considered to be by rail. In addition to the Sandia Laboratories, the Pantex Plant in Amarillo, Texas, discussed in Chapter Twenty-Seven, was a primary location for the manufacture of weapons and pits. The plant was constructed in 1941 as a munitions base, served through the Cold War and continues to serve nuclear weapons purposes today. As weapons and pits were built or refurbished, they were moved from the Pantex Plant to other bases

20. Nuclear Weapon Convoy Duty

for immediate use or to storage locations throughout the United States, including Manzano. Weapons were frequently moved from the plant to Charleston, SC, to supply the Navy ships and submarines in the Atlantic.

The DoE began to acquire used railroad cars and convert them into heavily armored boxcars and security guard cars. Referred to as Safe, Secure Railcars (SSRs) by the DoE, these cars provided a high degree of cargo protection in event of fire or serious accident and were fortified to resist an attack or any unauthorized entry. These trains pulled several armored boxcars sandwiched between special SSRs which had a cupola or turret on top. The cupola had small windows through which guards could keep an eye out for any potential problem and for use to protect the transported nuclear weapons, if necessary. The guards accompanying the assets were armed with rifles, automatic machine guns, and hand-grenade launchers.

Because of the cargo these trains carried, their maximum speed topped out at 35 to 40 m.p.h., making a cross-country trip very long and boring for the train crew and the accompanying security team. Consequently, one boxcar contained living quarters equipped with kitchen equipment, chairs, bunks, other appliances, security-sensitive instruments, and radios for the security guards who traveled with the weapons or birdcages.

These SSRs were originally painted white to be distinctive and were referred to as the "white trains." The 1094th Manzano Weapons Specialist also said, "They were definitely distinctive. They stuck out from all the other railroad cars." Realizing this white color could potentially pose a security problem, eventually the SSRs were painted a rusty looking railroad car color to make them less conspicuous, but the cupolas still made them easy to identify, as reflected in the photos below.

The green railcar with silver roof in the photo below was a former Boston and Maine baggage car, which became Amtrak Number 603, before it was sold to DoE. It was used to house materials and equipment but was never converted to white train specifications.

The anti-nuclear movement and public protests of nuclear weapons rail transportation developed into a serious security problem for the DoE. Not only did they produce negative publicity, they also

Part V—Base Security

The original white train SSR (Amarillo Railroad Museum).

The SSR repainted version (Amarillo Railroad Museum).

20. Nuclear Weapon Convoy Duty

A green railcar (Amarillo Railroad Museum).

brought public attention to what the DoE had planned to be a classified transportation process. In 1985, protests against the white trains reached the point where a change was required. The DoE, realizing there was no way to win the anti-nuclear fight, discontinued the use of railroads and began exclusively using overland Safeguard Transporters for moving nuclear materials.[1]

The use of the white trains came to an end in 1987, and what remains of the white trains are located at the Amarillo Railroad Museum, Amarillo, TX. A representative with the museum tells me these white train SSRs, armored cars, and a model S4 locomotive were donated to the museum by the Pantex Plant and were hauled to the museum by an American Locomotive Company (ALCO) switcher. The Burlington Northern and Santa Fe company (BNSF) had taken out the switch line to the museum property several years ago when it became inactive, so to get the cars to the museum BNSF installed curved rails from a nearby sideline and attached them to our rail line, and we rolled in the cars. Then BNSF reinstalled the rails back to their original location.

Part V—Base Security

Transportation by Aircraft

In 1948, the six engine B-36, seen in a photograph in Chapter Four, was a state-of-the-art plane and the first intercontinental bomber able to transport any weapon in the U.S. arsenal distances up to 3,900 miles. It was not originally designed to carry atomic weapons, and the required modifications were made by the HQ Squadron, 3170th Special Weapons Group at Kirtland. However, even with the modifications, loading the large MK17 thermonuclear weapon was a very long and time-consuming process. After modification, it was designated the B-36 B.

A 1094th air policeman stationed at Manzano in 1955 relates a story about convoying the pits to a waiting aircraft at Kirtland: "The birdcages containing the pit [the highly volatile weapon's trigger material discussed in Chapter Thirteen] were lined up down the aisle of a motor pool type school bus. Yes, that's what I said, a school bus! We convoyed the bus to the aircraft, usually a B-36 B from Biggs AFB in El Paso, parked on the Kirtland pads on the southside of the runway." Although transporting these volatile pits in a school bus seems like an unorthodox method, this story was corroborated by another AP stationed there in 1956–1960.

As the nuclear weapons increased in size, a different methodology was necessary to transport the weapon from Manzano to the Kirtland airfield. The air policeman continued, "In 1955, a straddle carrier resembling a lumber carrier [see photo on following page] was used to transport the MK 5, MK 6, and the larger MK 17 weapon. It was not unusual to have four straddle carriers in one convoy to planes waiting at Kirtland."

Once on the Kirtland pad, a security curtain was put up around the bomb bay doors, and the weapon was mechanically lifted into or removed from the bomb bay, as security guards stood around the aircraft at port arms. The air policeman said he found this somewhat paradoxical, considering that as the world's most lethal nuclear devices were being loaded or unloaded, people aboard the commercial airliners arriving and departing the same airport were totally unaware of the military activity taking place just a short distance from them.

20. Nuclear Weapon Convoy Duty

Straddle carrier (U.S. Air Force).

Transportation by Overland Trucks

In addition to using trains and aircraft, over-the-road transportation has been used extensively. Beginning in the 1950s, government owned or private trucking companies under contract to the government have transported nuclear weapons, nuclear components and materials, using 18-wheel tractor trailers, developed for and used by the NNSA. To oversee the process, the Transportation and Safeguards Division (TSD) was established in 1975 at the DoE's Albuquerque Operations Office and was subsequently renamed as the Office of Secure Transportation (OST) in the late 1990s. The TSD/OST is responsible for the safe and secure transport of government-owned special nuclear materials in the contiguous United States. To ensure the safe transport, the OST, through its sophisticated nationwide communication system in Albuquerque, NM, maintains real-time communication and monitors the status and location of each convoy. According to the NNSA, these cross-country drivers log over three and a half million miles each year and have a remarkable safety record. Although they have been involved in accidents, since its inception in 1975, there have been none that resulted in either a fatality or exposure of any radioactive material. That is a remarkable record.

Interestingly, many of the drivers are former military personnel; the OST attempts to hire military veterans, especially former special operation force members, or those experienced in high-risk armed tactical security work. This qualification is important because these drivers, and agents, may be called on to use deadly force to protect the assets being transported. The OST also recommends that drivers possess the ability to maneuver against a hostile adversary. During the transport, the trucks are accompanied by unmarked escort vehicles carrying OST agents.[2]

The Manzano Convoy Procedure

In 1964, the 1094th AP Squadron continued to provide the escort for the truck loaded with a nuclear weapon to or from Kirtland base or the secure railhead at Sandia Base. The weapon was removed from a structure or plant and loaded onto a special transport flatbed truck. The weapon was surrounded by a wood or metal frame and covered with a tarpaulin so the weapon was not visible. The convoy escort team waited at the secured "Q" area exit gate until the truck arrived and we initiated the escort procedure. Our escort convoy consisted of a guard riding in the truck with the driver, an advance vehicle, a lead vehicle, and a trail vehicle; each vehicle was manned with two people, armed with a M1 and a .45-caliber sidearm. Prior to leaving the Q Area, the convoy escort team was reminded that should the need arise in protecting the nuclear weapon, the use of deadly force was authorized.

The advance vehicle traveled ahead of the convoy, looking for anything suspicious on the road and under the arroyo bridge and ensuring the roadway was safe. If the advance vehicle team met oncoming traffic, it was their responsibility to get the oncoming vehicle off the road and clear the way for the convoy, because the convoy did not stop for anything. The lead vehicle traveled immediately

20. Nuclear Weapon Convoy Duty

ahead of the weapon truck, and the trail vehicle was close behind the truck. As specified by the DoD Directive previously mentioned, the security detail remained with the weapon until the security was passed to the aircraft group or a weapon was safely returned back to the secured area at Manzano.

The convoy route for transferring the weapons to the KUMMSC was the main road going to Manzano. An SF convoy commander tells me, "We ran a rolling detour to avoid meeting or passing normal traffic. Our group commander commissioned operators of a road grader, to prepare several parking areas along the route. The sweep team would direct or force any vehicle not part of the convoy, into these areas until the convoy cleared the areas, which was usually 10 to 15 minutes." The convoy commander said some people objected to being delayed; however, the base commander fully supported the procedure, knowing all SF people could be at risk if the asset (weapon) collided with any vehicle on the road.

Not only were the roads over which a weapon was transported a security concern but the air space as well. A plane produced little anxiety, but a helicopter possessed the ability to lift the weapon and transport it away, so they were considered a threat. To secure the air space, the aircraft control tower was informed of the convoy and requested to advise flight crews to remain clear of the area. The procedure for a convoy commander was to notify the command post of the planned convoy time and the call sign to be used. The convoy commander carried a special radio to keep the Command Post, the Base Command Post, and CSC advised of the convoy status.

A major and convoy commander tells me about an event that occurred in 1980:

> We were transporting a weapon from Manzano to a Kirtland flight line hot pad, and were well into the convoy route when I noticed a chopper approaching. I reported it to CSC and called the command post requesting them to warn the pilot not to overfly our position. The chopper continued its flight path directly toward the convoy, getting closer and closer. Not knowing how successful the command post or the control tower had been in making contact with the pilot, I instructed one of our four convoy armored vehicles to dismount and fire a flare to get the pilot's attention. The flare worked and the pilot immediately changed course. We were relieved because our next course of action would have been to fire at the tail rotor and disable the chopper. I knew our mission was to protect the weapon, but the thought of bringing down a chopper was a bit chilling as well. We later

Part V—Base Security

learned it was a HH53 combat search and rescue helicopter inbound to Kirtland from the McCormack Training Range south of the base.

We continued the convoy to Kirtland, and when we arrived, the wing commander was waiting. He had already contacted the 58th Special Operations Wing's Para Jumpers School about the incident. I did not participate in the ensuing conversations, but we did ask Base Command Post to update and record any planned priority movements, so the pilots would be aware of any scheduled convoy within the area in which they would be flying.

A first lieutenant security duty officer in the 1094th APS says this about the closing of the Killeen WSA in Texas in 1969: "We were running convoys way above the norm as weapons were being transferred into Manzano. We often worked weekdays from 1500 hours to 0800 hours the following morning, and on the weekends and holidays, 0800 hours one day to 0800 hours the following day."

After the Kirtland Underground Munitions Maintenance and Storage Complex (KUMSC), was activated in 1992, the 377th Security Forces Squadron at Kirtland had the responsibility to escort the convoys as the weapons were transferring from Manzano to the KUMSC. A special convoy flight was established to provide these escorts.

Part VI
Miscellaneous Manzano Information

21

Aircraft Crashes at Manzano

During its 42 years of operation, it appears that three confirmed aircraft crashes happened in the Manzano WSA. One involved a plane carrying a nuclear weapon, another crashing near weapons storage structures, and the third was an unidentified type of aircraft. The CSC (Central Security Control) Manzano area map shown in Appendix B indicates these crashes, and perhaps there are others of which we are not aware. Because of the nuclear weapons maintenance requirements previously discussed, accommodating planes carrying nuclear weapons into and out of Kirtland AFB was routine. Additionally, Kirtland was a refueling location for military aircraft, many of which were also carrying a nuclear weapon. Consequently, there were a lot of aircraft flying over the Manzano Mountains.

Manzano WSA is located just five miles SE of Kirtland and the Albuquerque International Sunport, a joint terminal serving both military and commercial airlines. At an elevation of 5,352 feet, the Sunport has three active runways averaging more than 419 daily flights in 2019, 40 percent of which were commercial and 16 percent military. The Albuquerque International Sunport map[1] indicates three active runways in close proximity to Manzano Base. The main east-west runway, number 8/26, was the runway from which two aircraft, a B-29 Superfortress and an F-100 C Super Sabre, departed prior to crashing at Manzano WSA.

Broken Arrows

The military term "broken arrow" is used to describe any incident in which a nuclear weapon is lost, stolen, otherwise

21. Aircraft Crashes at Manzano

unaccounted for, or inadvertently detonated. During the early years, modifying planes to carry these massive weapons—and learning how to effectively work with them—remained a challenge, and historians report that by November 10, 1950, five atomic bombs had been lost in accidents. During the Manzano active years, 1950–1992, there was one crash officially classified as a broken arrow, a B-29 Superfortress, transporting a nuclear weapon. The crash did not affect a storage structure because, as described in Chapter Eleven, the structures were designed and built to withstand a plane crash and avoid any potential problems associated with a nuclear weapon explosion. Detailed information relating to the crash is provided below. Another broken arrow was within the vicinity of Manzano when a B-36 dropped a bomb on its final landing approach to Kirtland.

B-29 Superfortress, April 11, 1950

A plane crash at Manzano involving a nuclear weapon occurred just seven days after the base became operational, becoming the second "broken arrow" on record. The first occurred earlier that year when a B-36 carrying a MK 4 nuclear weapon experienced a three-engine flameout and had to release and detonate the bomb at 3,000 feet, off the coast of Alaska. On April 11, 1950, at 2138 hours, a Silverplate B-29–100-BW Superfortress, registration number 45-21854, departed Kirtland AFB via runway eight. The B-29 had just taken on an atomic bomb and pit on a classified mission. According to aviation records, three minutes after takeoff and while beginning its initial climb, the aircraft went out of control and crashed on the north side of the Manzano mountain, approximately five and one-half miles east of the airfield, killing a crew of 13.

Loaded onboard the plane was a nuclear bomb, but fortunately, a nuclear explosion was avoided because the core or pit containing the nuclear material was not inserted into the bomb, a practice discussed in Chapter 13. According to historical records descriptions, the horizon became red, flames, visible for some 15 miles, shot upwards, and a violent explosion occurred. The bomb case was destroyed and some high-explosive components were burned in the fire. However, the detonators in the bomb sustained no damage, nor did the four spare detonators carried in a separate case. As a result of the containment, no contamination was discovered. All components recovered

Part VI—Miscellaneous Manzano Information

from the crash site were returned to the Atomic Energy Commission. The crash was officially listed as a "broken arrow." In typical reaction to any situation involving a nuclear weapon, the Air Force took control of the crash site and published a public statement that the B-29 was on a routine training flight out of Walker AFB, Roswell, NM, and had just refueled at Kirtland.

B-29 Superfortress crash site (U.S. government).

The official Army Air Force crash report has been declassified, and is available to the public. The crew of this plane was part of the 509th Bombardment Group with a history dating back to the 509th Composite Group and Lt. Col. Paul Tibbets, the pilot of the B-29 *Enola Gay* when it dropped

B-29 memorial monument (A1C Austin Prisbrey, Kirtland AFB Public Affairs).

21. Aircraft Crashes at Manzano

Little Boy, the first of two atomic bombs used in warfare on the Japanese city of Hiroshima.[2]

On April 11, 2019, in the foothills of the Manzano mountain, family members of the 13 airmen who lost their lives in the crash attended a memorial service and monument dedication. Although this area remains classified as Top Secret, a special access privilege was granted to the family members under a security escort. A military historian who assisted in the ceremony tells me that nobody asked any questions about what was beneath their feet. The monument, constructed in part using stones gathered from the crash site, displayed a plaque to honor the service of these airmen.

B-36 Peacemaker Drops a Hydrogen Bomb, May 22, 1957

Another broken arrow, not directly connected with Manzano but within close proximity, was when a hydrogen bomb accidentally fell from a B-36 aircraft. The aircraft (number 52–2816, call sign Spiral-16) was flying to Kirtland AFB from Biggs Army Air Field in Texas, on May 22, 1957, ferrying a MK 17 nuclear weapon, serial number 8053, when the accident occurred. As discussed in Chapter Ten, the MK 17, at 24 feet long, 61 inches in diameter, and 21 tons, was the largest nuclear weapon ever put into service by the United States, and the first droppable thermonuclear device. As previously indicated, the B-36 was one of the few aircraft large enough to carry the weapon, and even then, it required modifications. Loading the MK 17 into the B-36 was a very long and time-consuming process because the weapon had to be mechanically lifted into or removed from the bomb bay. This process no doubt created the possibility of several different types of mistakes.

The B-36 was on its final landing approach to Kirtland when the bomb fell through the bomb bay doors. The 1,700-foot drop was far too short a distance for its parachutes to open and slow its descent, so the impact was an earth-shattering explosion leaving a crater 12 feet deep, and 25 feet across. There was no nuclear reaction, but the non-nuclear high explosives in the bomb detonated with only minor radioactive contamination detected. Researchers believe the bomb would have had a nuclear explosive force of more than 10 million tons of TNT. On a comparison basis, the atomic bomb dropped on

Part VI—Miscellaneous Manzano Information

Hiroshima had a force equal to that of 16,000 tons of TNT. Luckily the MK 17 hit an uninhabited area owned by the University of New Mexico, but that location was just four and a half miles south of the Kirtland control tower.

No official reason was ever given as to why the accident occurred, but government documents relating to the crash indicate a safety release mechanism apparently had been moved to the wrong position. One speculation was that the first lieutenant who pulled the weapon locking pin lost his balance, and in trying to regain it grabbed for the nearest solid hand-hold, which unfortunately was a lever that gave way under his weight. Moving this lever triggered a succession of events, and the giant bomb pulled free from its mooring, tearing its way through the bomb bay doors. Another speculation was that a defectively designed release mechanism malfunctioned after the locking pin was removed, permitting the weapon to shift and fall.

For the following 24 years, no one knew about the incident. The government first acknowledged the accident in 1981 in a brief release saying only that a nuclear weapon of some kind had been dropped. It was not until August 1986, when the Associated Press, through the *Albuquerque Journal* newspaper, published an article based on information obtained through the Freedom of Information Act that the American public learned of this accident.[3]

Other Aircraft Crashes on Manzano

There have been other plane crashes on the "Manzano Mountains," and they are listed on various information sites. Unfortunately, most simply reference the Manzano Mountains, which could or could not be on the WSA itself. A third plane crash on the S/E side, inside the Q Area, is evident because plane fragments can be easily seen each afternoon as the sun reflects off them. Based on research, this was the crash of a USAF F-100 Super Sabre. I am also listing other aircraft crashes relating to Manzano, which I discovered during my research.

F-100C Super Sabre, August 1957

On August 10, 1957, a North American F-100C Super Sabre, MSN 54–1796 assigned to the 721st Fighter-Day Squadron (FDS),

21. Aircraft Crashes at Manzano

Foster AFB, Texas, crashed into the Manzano Mountains. The 721st Tactical Fighter Squadron was assigned to the 450th Tactical Fighter Wing at Foster. In 1954, the squadron became one of the first units to fly the North American F-86 Sabre, and the following year, the F-100 Super Sabre, the first USAF aircraft able to go supersonic in level flight. To reflect the F-100's air superiority capabilities, 1169 was inactivated with the closing of Foster AFB on December 18, 1958.

The official History of Flight states that 1st Lt. Delong was the flight leader of two F-100s on a scheduled proficiency cross country to include George AFB, Nellis AFB, Tinker AFB, Patterson AFB, and Myrtle Beach, South Carolina. After departing Foster AFB, the F-100C made an unscheduled stop at Kirtland because the pilot, Delong, realized the pylon fuel tanks were feeding too slowly. The tanks were inspected, and the fuel booster pumps were determined to be functioning satisfactorily. The plane was carefully preflighted, refueled, and departed Kirtland at 1506 MST. Once airborne, the landing gear would not properly retract, and the pylon tanks continued to feed slow. Lt. Delong began burning off fuel, and when the fuel level reached 2,000 pounds, he headed back to Kirtland to land. Unfortunately, eight miles from the base at 5,000 feet, an engine flameout occurred. Lt. Delong attempted an engine restart using the emergency fuel system, but it lasted only a few minutes before flaming out for the second time. Unable to land, the pilot turned toward the Manzano mountains. The primary cause for the crash was listed as engine flameout because of fuel starvation from an undetermined cause, with no contributing factors. According to Air Force records, this aircraft was put into service on September 24, 1955, and had 350 flight hours at the time of the crash. Several outstanding maintenance technical orders were cited as in a non-compliant status by the maintenance officer for this aircraft.

The flight history states the aircraft crashed at 1602 MST in an area east of Manzano Base, and the pilot safely ejected, landing on Manzano base. Could it be the writer of this report did not understand the configuration of the Manzano WSA, and distinguished the "Administrative Area" as the base, separate from the "area East of Manzano Base?" I suspect this to have a high probability, and the F-100 was, in fact, the third crash.[4]

Part VI—Miscellaneous Manzano Information

Navy P-51, 1951

Interestingly, a crash site is shown on a Manzano CSC area wall map (see Appendix B), identified, as best I can read this almost illegible writing, as "mAG fjcm Navy P 51, 1951, 0 dead." The location of this crash site on the map is east of the Q Area access point, southeast of Saddle Road, across from structures numbered 58 and 59. In my research of Navy or military crashes, and crashes in New Mexico or Albuquerque, I found no record of a P-51 aircraft crash. In the absence of an aircraft number, additional information cannot be obtained. Whether or not the crashed aircraft was a P-51 or if the information on the wall map was accurate is debatable, and I can neither prove nor disprove the validity of either one.

RB-57-CF, June 27, 1972

Another crash in the Manzano Mountains involved a Martin/General Dynamics RB-57F-CF, in which both crew members were killed. The RB-57, number 13293, MSN 173, was assigned to 58th Weather Reconnaissance Squadron. The 58th Reconnaissance Squadron, originally activated February 15, 1954, was last assigned to the 9th Weather Reconnaissance Wing at Kirtland AFB and was equipped with 12 RB-57F Canberra reconnaissance aircraft. The Martin/General Dynamics RB-57F was a specialized strategic reconnaissance aircraft developed in the 1960s for the United States Air Force from the Martin B-57 Canberra tactical bomber. Part of the duties of the 58th involved high-altitude atmospheric sampling and radiation detection work in support of nuclear test monitoring. The 58th was inactivated June 30, 1974. Beyond the listing of this crash on an American military aircraft website known for its accuracy, I cannot locate any information. Even an aviation archaeological research site has no information.[5]

EC 135 Tactical Air Command Jet, September 14, 1977

On September 14, 1977, an 8th Tactical Deployment Control Squadron EC 135 Air Command Jet, registration number 62–3536, crashed into the Manzano Mountains shortly after takeoff from runway eight. The EC 135 was a modified Boeing C-135 Stratolifter,

21. Aircraft Crashes at Manzano

which served as a 24-hour-a-day flying command post for the Strategic Air Command during the Cold War. Under a program titled Looking Glass, the EC 135 flew continuously from February 3, 1961, until it ceased continuous airborne alert status on July 24, 1990, logging over 281,000 hours in the air. The EC 135, based at Seymour Johnson AFB, Goldsboro, NC, was en route to Nellis AFB, NV, to participate in an Army training exercise. It had just made a scheduled refueling stop at Kirtland AF and was attempting to become airborne again just prior to 2400 hours. It took off on runway eight, an east-west runway with a progressively rising terrain toward the Manzano Mountains, some five miles away. The official AF crash report reflects the flight path of the aircraft from Kirtland to the crash site.

It was speculated the crew was fatigued and possibly ignored the normal departure and climb procedures. Other information I located came from an individual stationed at Kirtland, who said he read the accident report in 1983. He stated the report indicated that, after refueling, the amount of fuel on the aircraft was more than the crew realized. The weight of this excess fuel produced erroneous data used to calculate the takeoff and roll information. Additionally, because the pilot was flying in the dark and in unfamiliar terrain, he may not have realized the mountains were so close to Kirtland. According to reports, air traffic control advised the pilot about the low altitude, and instructed him to turn right and increase altitude immediately. There was, however, no radio transmission from the pilot indicating a problem. If the plane lacked sufficient power to climb above the mountain and avoid the rapidly rising terrain, the pilot apparently was too busy trying to fly the plane, since he never reported any problem. The crash investigation indicated there were no technical problems or no structural, or electrical system failure.

Debris was scattered across 10 acres on the north side of the mountain. An official photo indicates the crash site was about 32 feet below the summit of the mountain. Two nuclear storage bunkers were located on the access road inside the Q Area, in the vicinity of the crash site. One book contributor, a major with the 1606th Security Police Squadron, tells me he was there at the time of this crash and well remembers all the fuel that burned up between the two bunkers. No official cause for the crash has been publicly disclosed.[6]

Part VI—Miscellaneous Manzano Information

All 20 occupants of the plane were killed in the crash. Among those in the crash was Col. Harlan Hume, vice commander, 1st Special Operations Wing, who flew more than 100 missions during the Vietnam War and had been awarded four Distinguished Flying Crosses. Also killed was Col. Keith Grimes, a weatherman who provided a weather forecast of moonlight and ideal weather conditions for the infamous raid on the North Vietnamese POW camp Son Tay in November 1970. In that raid, between 100 and 200 North Vietnamese casualties were estimated, but no POWs were found in the camp. Intelligence later revealed that the POWs at Son Tay had been moved to a camp 15 miles away the previous July. Despite this intelligence failure, the raid was deemed a "tactical success" due to its nearly flawless execution. For their actions during the raid, the members of the task force were awarded six Distinguished Service Crosses, five Air Force Crosses, and 83 Silver Stars.[7]

Air Force Rescue personnel arrived on crash scene and enlisted the assistance of the Manzano Security Force to locate human remains and belongings. As remains were retrieved, a temporary morgue was set up in an abandoned bowling alley just outside the fence line, as the medical team attempted to identify victims.

22

Wildlife and Varmints on the Mountain

Wildlife was plentiful on the mountains and often reminded us that it was their mountain first. The wildlife included coyotes, bobcats, rabbits, several species of snakes and, of course, tarantulas.

On night patrol, it was nothing unusual to drive around a curve and see two green eyes glowing as the truck headlights shined on the varmint. They disappeared quickly, and we resumed our patrol. That was not much of a concern because we always remained in the truck. I never knew anyone with enough grit to pursue a varmint. On the midnight shift, we made our first patrol round checking the seal on each structure. That involved getting out of the truck, walking to the structure door, directing the flashlight on the seal to verify its authenticity. Standing at the structure door in the total darkness and hearing a howl or cry close by made one a bit uncomfortable. We completed the structure check as quickly as possible and let the varmints roam freely.

A 1094th SP related a story from back in 1955 when he and his patrol partner were on the backside of the mountain near the Sierra Area. His partner, who was riding shotgun, spotted a bobcat about 100 yards away and asked him to stop the truck. His partner got out, raised his M1 rifle and fired, and being an expert shot, he killed it in one shot. His partner was about six-foot-two, and when he held the bobcat by the tail and lifted it up, its head touched the ground. That was a big bobcat. I asked if his partner suffered any repercussions for firing his weapon while on duty, and the answer was no. The personnel who checked in the weapons did not count rounds of ammunition, so one ammo clip was turned in with only six cartridges, not the full seven. In 1964 when I was stationed there, you best not fire your rifle. At the end of our shift, when we turned in our M-1 and

Part VI—Miscellaneous Manzano Information

.45 pistols, the weapons checker would check each clip to verify it contained the required number of cartridges and sniff to see it the weapon had been fired. If it had been fired, rest assured there would be hell to pay.

There are at least four natural springs and seeps on the Manzano Mountains within the "Q" area. One is located on the northeast corner close to the intersect of Alpha and Bravo sectors. Before I arrived in 1964, someone put several goldfish in that spring and APs fed the fish on a regular basis. The goldfish had evidently been there for some time, because a few appeared to be 12 to 15 inches long. They were beautiful fish, and it was always a good feeling to climb the mountain and feed them before the sun went down on a swing shift. That experience provided a bit of serenity in the rugged, desolate, and dry mountain terrain. Don't know how long they lasted, but they were there when I left in 1966.

Another AP stationed there in 1953 said one friendly rock miner working on the tunnels related a story about a mountain lion that lived somewhere in the four hills area of Manzano. An AP shot and killed the lion. That is the only story I heard about a lion living on the mountain, but I guess it could be true.

Coyotes were seen on the mountain regularly, especially at night when they were hunting for food. We left them alone, and they left us alone, but we often heard their cries.

Bull snakes abound in this climate. These nonvenomous snakes are usually docile but can be quite defensive if provoked. When a bull snake detects live objects too big to be prey, they perceive the object as a predator and take defensive action. Their first reaction is to remain docile, not making any movement. Then, when they feel they are able to flee from the object, their defense is to move away as quickly as possible. Adult bull snakes average about four to six feet in length, and because of their markings, they are often mistaken for western diamondback rattlers.

Tarantulas were plentiful on the mountain, and many of them grow as large as the palm of a human hand. These big, beefy, hairy spiders strike fear in the hearts of most people, when in fact, they are some of the least aggressive and least dangerous spiders around. Tarantulas are quite passive, rarely bite, and unless a person is highly allergic to their venom, their bite is no worse than a bee sting in terms of toxicity.

22. Wildlife and Varmints on the Mountain

Rattlesnakes were plentiful on the mountain, and most people went out of their way to avoid them. The snake owned the space they occupied, and no one wanted to challenge that. However, there always seem to be a few people who throw caution to the wind. A 1094th AP, who told the story about the guy who killed the bobcat, said the same man had an encounter with a rattlesnake while patrolling the perimeter road. The airman spotted a three- to four-foot-long Western Diamondback crawling on the side of the road, got out of the truck, and proceeded to pick it up by the head. He then milked the snake's venom on the bumper of the truck and turned it loose. His partner said he stood way back from all that action, as most of us would. I am not sure the airman was into herpetology, but apparently, he possessed no ophidiophobia.

The varmints had a way of keeping us in touch with reality by reminding us that danger on the mountain was always present, whether it was nuclear, human or wildlife, and the possibility for something to happen could never be discounted.

23

Manzano's Aerial Phenomena

Any aerial phenomenon that cannot immediately be identified or explained is often referred to as an Unidentified Flying Object (UFO). The term has been around since the U.S. Air Force first coined it in 1953 to serve as a catch-all for anything they could not or would not explain. During the Cold War, any unidentified aircraft or anomaly on the radar was commonly referred to as a "Bogey," indicating a potential enemy plane in the area. During peacetime, that same type anomaly is casually referred to as a UFO or an unexplained aerial phenomenon (UAP). Often there is a logical explanation, while on other occasions the explanation is not considered credible.

During the past 75 years, UFO/UAP activity has occurred near sites associated with nuclear storage, weaponry and technology. According to information, Sandia Base, Los Alamos, Livermore, and Savannah River have all experienced dramatic incidents of unknown types of aircraft appearing and hovering above their facilities. No one seems to know from where they came or their purpose in being there. As one example, in late 1948, green balls were spotted in the sky near the Los Alamos National Laboratory and Sandia Base, where the atomic bomb was developed. This repeated activity around our most sensitive defense sites prompts scientists and military to speculate whether they may originate from our known or unknown adversaries.

Given the secrecy surrounding Manzano Base and the covert activities conducted behind the fences, it is not surprising that over the years the base has been linked to UFO sightings and conspiracy theories. These sightings appear to cover an extended period of time from possibly as far back as the 1940s into 1992 and are relatively consistent in nature. These UFO sightings were reported by not only military personnel but also by Albuquerque residents. Several of these UFO sightings have been publicized by the National

23. Manzano's Aerial Phenomena

Unidentified flying objects at Manzano (Norio Hayakawa).

Investigations Committee on Aerial Phenomena, a privately supported fact-finding group, including these selected incidents below.

- On August 25, 1951, a Sandia Base security guard saw a wing-shaped craft flying at 800 to 1,000 feet, without making a sound. He estimated the size of the aircraft at one and one-half times the size of a B-36 wingspan or about 350 feet and its speed at 300 to 400 mph. It had six pairs of soft glowing lights on the underside and remained visible for about 30 seconds.
- On June 5, 1952, a SSgt at Kirtland AFB saw a shiny round object flying much faster than an F-86 jet fighter for about six seconds before disappearing in the night sky.
- On June 8, 1952, at 10:50 a.m., two Albuquerque residents witnessed four shiny objects flying straight and level in a diamond formation for several seconds.
- On July 26, 1952, at 12:05 a.m., an airman at Kirtland saw eight to 10 orange balls flying very fast in a "V" formation for five seconds.

Several articles have been published concerning UFO sightings in and around Manzano and Kirtland bases back in 1980. I also located a couple of additional interesting articles.

Part VI—Miscellaneous Manzano Information

- An article in the USAF Project Blue Book[1] relates this incident. On November 4, 1957, two Kirtland air traffic controllers saw a 15 to 20 foot, egg-shaped object in the sky with a white light at its base. This highly maneuverable object crossed the flight line, taxiways, and runways, flying in the direction of the tower. It was flying about 50 m.p.h. just 20 to 30 feet above ground, until it reached the NE corner of the restricted Manzano Nuclear Weapons Storage Area and the B-58 bomber crash site, where it hovered for approximately one minute, then headed East again.
- One web site provides this UFO information: Around 1979–1980, there were two reported UFO incidents at Manzano, where these unidentified craft landed inside the fenced-off perimeter despite the security of the base. However, after further research, one UFO enthusiast came to the conclusion that those two incidents were most likely drone technology. Perhaps some military unit was testing out how easy it would be to breach Manzano. The AFOSI agent Richard Doty was responsible for the investigation and completing the paperwork for those two incidents.[2]

Paul Bennewitz, an American businessman and UFO investigator, owned a company named Thunder Scientific, which was located adjacent to Kirtland Air Force Base. On several occasions late at night or in the early morning hours, Mr. Bennewitz said he witnessed strange, unidentified objects flying over Kirtland and the nearby Manzano Mountains. These could have been a type of military advanced technological developmental aircraft, but for Mr. Bennewitz, they were alien craft or UFOs. In 1979, Mr. Bennewitz was certain he was receiving communications from alien spacecraft within the vicinity of Albuquerque. In the 1980s, he was convinced he had located a secret underground base near Dulce, NM, near the Colorado border. The theory became known as the Dulce Base. Adding to the support of such alien activities, several residents of Dulce claim to have seen moving lights in the sky, along with other sights for which they had no explanation.[3]

Political scientist Michael Barkun wrote in his book *A Culture of Conspiracy: Apocalyptical Visions in Contemporary America* that abandoned, former Cold War underground missile installations gave

23. Manzano's Aerial Phenomena

plausibility to the Dulce Base rumors.[4] If abandoned underground missile installations could house this type of activity, could the storage structures, such as the ones at Manzano, ostensibly not do the same? Bennewitz advocated a connection between Dulce and Manzano Base, and it was his contention that because of the underground complex tunneled into the mountains, Manzano would be a likely extension of the Dulce Base. Bennewitz claimed to have made contact with an alien presence at Manzano, and in 1979, documented an alien culture that had been present underground at Manzano.

Over the years, several sighting incidents have been published concerning UFOs at Manzano. Here are just a few of those.

According to one source, on November 4, 1957, at approximately 2245 hours, air traffic controllers at Kirtland picked up an egg-shaped object on radar circling over the base at an estimated speed of 150 to 200 m.p.h., and then descending as if it were going to land on runway 26. Instead of landing, the object crossed the flight line and headed toward the NE corner of Manzano Base where it hovered for about one minute, then turned into a steep climb. The object disappeared from the radar and then reappeared some 20 minutes later following a C-46, which had just taken off, for 15 miles or so before it went off scope.[5]

Another incident occurred on August 9, 1980. As a security policeman (SP) worked routine patrol, he was dispatched to respond to an ADT alarm. Upon arriving, the patrolman saw a bright light behind the structure and what appeared to be a disk-shaped, round object. The patrolman's vehicle radio was inoperable, so he decided to approach the disk on foot. When getting closer, the object lifted off in a vertical directional and sped away at a high rate of speed. Indications are the SP reported the incident to the Office of Special Investigations at Kirtland to be investigated. A preliminary report was filed, but no follow up final report was ever published. Why? Strong evidence indicates that a final report was completed but is being intentionally withheld from publication by the Air Force.

On an unknown date, a UFO sighting was reported by an SP about 0200 or 0300 hours while working a midnight shift. He was on main gate duty and noticed a blue light or flare streak shoot above him. He reported it to his flight commander, as he thought he should do. After the shift was over, he was informed the Security and

Part VI—Miscellaneous Manzano Information

Intelligence personnel wanted to speak to him about his report of a UFO. They very nicely instructed him to keep his mouth shut and not discuss the incident with anyone. Additionally, he was restricted to the base for the next five days. He heard nothing else about the incident and certainly didn't say any more about it.

While on patrol in Charlie Sector, on August 8, 1980, about 2350 hours, three SPs observed a bright light traveling at a great speed on the east side of Manzano, near Coyote Canyon. It stopped and hovered for a short time, then took off almost straight up at a high speed, disappearing into the night. They decided not to say anything, since they were working under the Air Force Personnel Reliability Program, a DoD evaluation program for military personnel with duties tied to nuclear weapons, to ensure they are reliable to perform nuclear-related responsibilities. Filing a report could subject them to criticism and possible dismissal from the program, which meant being removed from SP duty.[6]

Robert Hastings, a researcher of UFO incidents,[7] interviewed an SP who said that in 1992, while working at Manzano, he and three other SPs spotted a triangular craft in the sky with no lights and moving slowly. They watched for 15 to 20 seconds, and the craft turned and sped out of sight. Being advised not to call it in or say anything about their sighting for fear of repercussions, they didn't speak of it again. He also said he heard other unreported stories of the same nature that dated back into the 1940s.

Were these sightings a comet or a bright meteor, perhaps an atmospheric optical phenomenon, or could they have really been UFOs? Possibly, but considering all the activity at Sandia and Kirtland, it is very likely these UFOs could have been planes or weapons being tested. Although not much has been published concerning the development of experimental weapons, one bit of information was made public in July 2020 with the declassification of "A Site Report for Kirtland Air Force Base" in 2008. This report disclosed that in 1969, the Sandia Optical Range, at Sandia Base, was selected as the location for development and testing of a Gas Dynamic Laser (GDL). Atoms would be electrified within this high-energy laser, resulting in a beam of light exiting at a nozzle. The purpose of the GDL testing was to determine the possibility of using lasers as a substitute for conventional weapons. In 1972, the GDL was paired with a telescope to test the possibility of permitting it to be directed toward a moving

23. Manzano's Aerial Phenomena

target. The combined devices were used to successfully hit an aerial target in 1973.[8]

Remember, as we previously noted, Kirtland's Air Research and Development Command's primary mission, in conjunction with the Atomic Energy Commission, Sandia Laboratories, and Los Alamos National Laboratory, was to analyze, create, and test weapons involving aircraft. Today this includes airborne LASER weapons, particle beams, plasma weapons, and who knows what else.

UFOs, experimental aircraft, or Star Wars weapons? Perhaps we will never know.

24

Abandoned in Place

The deactivation and closing of weapons storage areas (WSA) was the result of two major considerations for the military, each with an interconnection to the other. First, with the de-escalation of nuclear weapons came the need to reduce the number of weapons built and maintained. Second was the need for a substantial reduction in military budgets, even at the expense of the nuclear program. After consideration of the prospect of ever-increasing military spending with no constraint in sight, the conclusion was reached in Congress that there must be a sharp cutback in the defense budget, with a major realignment of priorities. A plan was to be developed for appropriate base closures, and related economies, required to reduce the budget.

First Consideration: The De-Escalating of Nuclear Weapons

In addition to the nuclear weapons stockpiled within the United States, in April 1954, President Eisenhower authorized U.S. air bases operating in the United Kingdom, Germany, and Morocco to receive and store nuclear weapons, including the thermonuclear bomb. From the mid–1950s through 1990, some 13,000 nuclear weapons were deployed outside the continental United States to reinforce the country's security commitment to allies around the world. The Pentagon anticipated this deployment tactic would indicate to any adversary that military action against a U.S. ally carried the risk of escalating into a nuclear war.[1]

However, there was then, and remained for several years, a non-consensus of opinion about deploying nuclear weapons overseas.

24. Abandoned in Place

While the Eisenhower administration was confident in sharing nuclear weapons with its NATO allies, his successor, John Kennedy, had many reservations. One of President Kennedy's greatest fears was that someone might gain unauthorized access to a weapon and use it without his knowledge or consent. He wanted assurances that could not happen. To solve the problem, Sandia Laboratories developed a solution to improve presidential control. The program, termed Permissive Action Links, was deemed a major contributor to global security through better control of nuclear weapons in overseas locations. Now, everyone could breathe a little easier.[2]

By the mid–1960s both the United States and the Soviet Union had enough nuclear power to completely obliterate each other. Knowing this capability existed produced a mutual respect because both sides knew an attack upon the other would have catastrophic results for them. This realization created a time out, referred to in 1971 as "détente," for a period of improved relations between the United States and the Soviet Union. It was a time period to reduce the possibility of nuclear conflict, which loomed over the world like a dark cloud. Speaking at the 1976 Republican National Convention in Kansas City, the defeated Republican nominee, Ronald Reagan, proclaimed, "We live in a world in which the great powers have poised and aimed at each other, horrible missiles of destruction that can, in a matter of minutes, arrive in each other's country and destroy virtually the civilized world we live in."[3] During the 1980s, the relations between the United States and the Soviet Union improved dramatically, as Mikhail Gorbachev assumed control of the Soviet Union and announced a new era of restructuring and openness. During a November 1985 Geneva summit, President Reagan and Mr. Gorbachev met privately in the meeting location's estate pool house to discuss eliminating entire classes of nuclear weapons. In October 1986, Gorbachev proposed a 50 percent reduction of nuclear weapons for both the United States and Soviet Union. Unfortunately, because of issues over President Reagan's Space Defense Initiative, which could not be resolved, the Soviet Union refused the proposal and instead, the Intermediate Nuclear Forces Treaty was signed on December 8, 1987, eliminating an entire class of nuclear weapons.

With the Cold War now some 40 years old, dramatic economic and social changes were occurring in the Soviet Union. Its influence was diminishing, and it was unable to maintain control of its

Part VI—Miscellaneous Manzano Information

individual states. The first president of the Russian Federation, Boris Yeltsin, in his December 1991 speech acknowledged the Cold War had ended, and on December 26, 1991, the Soviet Union officially dissolved, breaking into 15 separate nations. With the end of the Cold War, the United States and Russia reduced spending on nuclear weapons, although both countries continued to maintain significant stocks of nuclear missiles.

Over the years, many U.S. government officials, members of congress and military leaders have advocated for, and embraced the concept of, a world free of nuclear weapons. The term denuclearization was coined to describe the process leading to a complete nuclear disarmament. However, as would be expected, there were two diametrically opposed opinions about denuclearization. Opponents insisted it would undermine any possibility to deter a nuclear war, while the protagonist hypothesized it would reduce the probability of a nuclear war, especially through non-intentional action. Those two perspectives promoted many disarmament negotiations, and several treaties have been signed in an effort to reduce the number of nuclear weapons possessed by the United States, Russia, and other countries. Those treaties included the following.[4]

- 1963 *Partial Test Ban Treaty* prohibited nuclear weapon testing except underground.
- 1968 (effective 1970) *Nuclear Non-Proliferation Treaty* was an international treaty to limit the spread of nuclear weapons.
- 1972 *Interim Agreement on Offensive Arms* (SALT I) had the United States and Soviet Union agree to a freeze in the number of intercontinental, and submarine-launched, ballistic missiles.
- 1979 *Strategic Arms Limitation Treaty* (SALT II), replacing SALT I, limited the Americans and Soviets to an equal number of ICBM launchers, SLBM launchers, and heavy bombers.
- 1987 *Intermediate-Range Nuclear Forces Treaty* created a global ban on short- and long-range nuclear weapons systems.
- 1991 (ratified 1994) *Strategic Arms Reduction Treaty* (START I) limited long-range nuclear forces in the United States, and the newly independent states of the former Soviet Union, to 6,000 attributed warheads on 1,600 ballistic missiles and bombers.

24. Abandoned in Place

- 1993 *Strategic Arms Reduction Treaty II* (START II) was a bilateral agreement between the United States and Russia which attempted to commit each side to deploy no more than 3,000 to 3,500 warheads by December 2007. It was never put into force.
- 1996 *Comprehensive Test Ban Treaty* was an international treaty to ban all nuclear explosions in all environments. While the treaty is not enforced, Russia has not tested a nuclear weapon since 1990 and the United States has not since 1992.
- 2002 *Strategic Offensive Reduction Treaty* (SORT) saw Russia and the United States agree to reduce their "strategic nuclear warheads" to between 1,700 and 2,200 by 2012. It was superseded by New START Treaty
- 2011 *New START Treaty* replaced SORT treaty, to reduce deployed nuclear warheads by about half, and will remain into force until at least 2021.
- 2017 *Treaty on the Prohibition of Nuclear Weapons* prohibited possession, manufacture, development, and testing of nuclear weapons, or assistance in such activities, by parties of the treaty.

Many of these treaties involved years of negotiations, and although not totally successful, they appeared to have resulted in important steps in both arms reductions, and mitigating the risk of nuclear war. As a result of these treaties, the U.S. nuclear weapon stockpile decreased from 23,368 weapons in 1985 to 7,260 in 2014, and the Soviet Union decreased from 39,197 in 1985 to 7,500 in 2014.

During the time period 1979 to 1993 as treaties were being negotiated, these weapons were being systematically removed from those bases and returned to the mainland to ultimately be decommissioned and dismantled. Many of these weapons were transferred to Manzano, and public data in 1991 estimated that approximately 2,092 warheads were stored in the Manzano WSA.

How many weapons were involved in this overseas removal process remains unknown. Since inception, the government has considered the deployment of nuclear weapons overseas, and the arrangements surrounding their placement, as top secret. In fact, resources indicate even members of Congress had difficulty getting

Part VI—Miscellaneous Manzano Information

information. Although the military has released limited overseas deployment information on occasion over the years, the DoE and the DoD have diligently worked to keep the information classified, demonstrating the rigid approach that has been taken to protect the secrecy of historical nuclear deployments.[5]

Ironically, this nuclear weapons decommissioning increased the role of the Kirtland base as a nuclear storage area, creating the need for the new Kirtland Underground Munitions Storage Complex.

Second Consideration: The Military Budget

After World War II ended and the Cold War was evolving into a full-scale operation, serious consideration was given to U.S. response capabilities should the Soviets begin a nuclear war. Military analysts were continuously comparing American and Soviet strategic weapons stockpiles and playing the numbers game to make a case for increased military spending. Unfortunately, trying to stay ahead of each other had wreaked havoc on the economy and budgets of both countries. In 1950, the State Department and the Department of Defense drafted a report (NSC-68), which was the initial framework establishing a formal U.S. Cold War Policy specific to the Soviet Union and its allies, and presented it to President Harry Truman. This report assessed the U.S. objectives as poorly implemented, proclaiming "present programs and plans ... dangerously inadequate." It emphasized the need for covert operations and mandated a significant increase in U.S. intelligence-gathering capabilities. The United States would rise to eliminate the report's assertions of inadequacy, but it would be costly. The report recommended tripling defense spending to $40 or $50 billion per year from the original $13 billion set for 1950, a proposal which, needless to say, met with great resistance in Congress.[6]

President Truman wanted to curb military spending even after the Soviets became a nuclear power, but rather than rejecting outright the report recommendations, he instead requested additional information on the estimate of costs involved. However, when North Korean forces, with support from the Chinese and Soviets, crossed the 38th parallel on June 25, 1950, NSC 68 took on new importance. Manzano Base, which had just been activated as a WSA, became a major player in the nuclear weapon buildup in 1950. Dwight Eisenhower succeeded Truman as president in 1953 and was instrumental in guiding the greatest military buildup, and intelligence surveillance, in U.S. history at that time, even as cost continued to increase. In his 1961 farewell address President Eisenhower made the statement, "We spend annually on military security more than the net income of all U.S. corporations."[7] By 1969, the U.S. military defense budget increased to $80.77 billion, representing 44 percent of the total U.S. budget, and was expected to continue increasing, causing alarms at many government levels. The 1969 military budget is interesting considering that, for fiscal year 2021, the budget for just the Department of the Air Force was $169 billion. Between 1940 and 1996, the total amount spent by the United States on all nuclear weapons programs is estimated to be $5.5 trillion.

The escalating cost of developing and maintaining the nuclear program and its support groups continued to have a great impact on the military budget. As the initial budget reduction and efficiency effort began, Killeen Base WSA, designated as Site Baker, in Texas, was the first WSA to be closed. Originally built in the late 1940s, it was deactivated in December 1969. All weapons were transferred to other locations, and the base was turned over to the Army and renamed West Fort Hood. In early 1970, President Richard Nixon signed an executive order creating a DoD Blue-Ribbon commission to investigate the possibility of closing or consolidating Sandia Base and Kirtland. A study was conducted to determine whether Manzano should be included in the consolidation or remain as a separate base under the control of DASA. Although Sandia, Manzano, and Kirtland bases were interconnected and worked cohesively in the nuclear weapons program, they operated independently, with individual budgets.

The Recommendation: Consolidate and Reorganize

As a result of the recommendations in the DoD's Commission Blue-Ribbon Panel report, on March 29, 1971, Deputy Secretary of Defense David Packard announced the reorganization of DASA to become effective July 1, 1971. Pursuant to that reorganization plan, under DoD Directive 5105.31,[8] on November 3, 1971, DASA became

Part VI—Miscellaneous Manzano Information

the Defense Nuclear Agency (DNA) with two objectives. First, its functions would be limited to nuclear weapon management, testing, and effects research. Second, Kirtland Air Force Base, Sandia Base, and Manzano Base would be consolidated under Air Force Systems Command (AFSC), with the transfer of most of the nuclear functions to Kirtland. In turn, Kirtland was charged with the responsibility to maintain the ability to deliver nuclear weapons to war-fighters to protect the nation and its allies.[9]

The Logistics of Consolidation

The logistics of merging three military bases together must have been a tremendous undertaking, and every unit, irrespective of its function, was impacted, including administration, medical, security, motor pool, weapons maintenance, dining room, service clubs, etc. It is impossible to include the impact to all these different units in this discussion, but I want to focus on the security police consolidation process. This involved combining not only two AF Security Police Squadrons but also the Military Police Squadron at Sandia. They were two distinctly different groups with two different operating processes and procedures. That was quite a challenge.

According to an unpublished historical document provided by the Kirtland AFB historian, a merger meeting was convened on May 13, 1971, attended by seven individuals representing the three bases: a colonel from AFSC; two representatives each from the Sandia Provost Marshal's office and security police and administration at Kirtland; and two members of the Manzano Security Police Squadron, a captain, director of security, and a captain, assistant chief of security police, who are contributors to this book. I am certain the meeting was a thorough discussion of milestones to be achieved, and the related tasks necessary to achieve each one. The meeting document[10] includes some 29 milestones agreed upon, and I have included several of those below to highlight the significant milestones they were challenged to meet in this consolidation.

- Functions and personnel of Manzano and Sandia Military Police will be consolidated into AFSWC, and Security Police Division from Kirtland and Manzano will be housed on Sandia Base.

24. Abandoned in Place

- Weapons storage will be in two locations, Manzano and Sandia. All Kirtland weapons storage will be transferred to Sandia.
- Operational control of Sandia and Manzano will be under the AFSWC Security Police. Military Police at Sandia will be phased out over a one-year period.
- The ranking Army officer will discipline the Army personnel, and the same will apply to the AF Security Police personnel.
- A security officer will stay at Manzano. All security will emanate from the Manzano Central Security Control location.
- The Law Enforcement function will remain basically the same. Military Police and Security Police flights will be combined.
- There will be two separate locations for Pass and Registration: one at Sandia entrance on Gibson, and the present one at Kirtland.
- Investigation Office will be consolidated and run out of Sandia.
- There will be a detention facility at Sandia.
- All posts will be operated jointly by Army and Air Force personnel, but in accordance with Air Force regulations.
- Traffic Control will continue to be operated by Military Police, and will continue to use the Traffic Section manned by Army personnel. Air Force personnel will slowly be phased in.

On merger/consolidation day, July 1, 1971, the Air Force Special Weapons Center (AFSWC), a subsidiary unit under the Air Force Systems Command (AFSC), assumed charge of Kirtland AFB, and jurisdiction over Manzano. The AFSC transferred the Manzano maintenance plants and storage structures facilities to the new 3098th Aviation Depot Squadron of the AF Logistics Command (AFLC), replacing the old Manzano 1094th Aviation Group. According to the base consolidation plan, base traditional support functions for Manzano base were provided by the 4900th Air Base Wing (ABW) at Kirtland. The 4900th APS assumed the responsibility for security, and members of the Manzano 1094th Air Police Squadron were consolidated into the 4900th SPS.[11] With the change to the

Part VI—Miscellaneous Manzano Information

4900th also came a change in the security patrol organization. To protect the base and provide for additional security requirements during the weapons transfer process, the old 1094th configuration of six flights of nine people each was changed to four flights of 18 to 22 people per flight. Also, during this time frame, the "15 in five" security procedures were implemented, boosting the manpower requirements for the mountain significantly. The 15 in five simply meant that a team of 15 men were charged to respond to any alarm within five minutes. An SP Lt. Colonel tells me that because of the distance around the mountain, two 15 in five teams were required.

Kirtland's command changed again in 1977 when the Military Airlift Command (MAC) took control, inactivating the 4900th ABW and replacing it with the Air Force Systems Command 1606th Air Base Wing. In 1978, the 1606th was separated into two units: the 1606th Security Police Squadron was responsible for law enforcement, flight line, and administration, and the 1608th Security Police Squadron assumed responsibility for Manzano base security. The 1608th SPS felt self-satisfied in their protection of Manzano, as we did in the old 1094th APS. One 1608th SPS member made the observation that the 1608 SPS took great pride in being the peacekeepers of the Manzano Weapons Storage Area, knowing that the job we do in securing this huge restricted area makes our world a little safer to live in.

Although Kirkland officially took over the command and control of Manzano Base in 1971, the majority of nuclear weapons day-to-day functions remained in place. The weapons storage structures continued to be used, but the routine service and maintenance work performed at the four Manzano plants was consolidated into plants number III and IV. The work at these plants remained in use until the total activity was transferred to the new weapons storage complex at Kirtland. To direct the security activities while nuclear weapons continued to be stored at Manzano, the 4900th SPS used the CSC/ADT room, located in plant Portal A (discussed in Chapter Eighteen), as a communications center from 1971 through October 1992. Sandia Laboratories continued to use Plant II for testing and storage.

Because of the merger and the development of the Kirtland Underground Munitions Maintenance and Storage Complex (KUMMSC), the need to use and maintain the plants and storage structures at Manzano was progressively reduced. When KUMMSC

24. Abandoned in Place

was ready to receive weapons for storage, an estimated 2,092 weapons were transferred from Manzano. The combat-decorated 377th Air Base Wing was re-activated to become the new host unit of Kirtland Air Force Base, and the 377th Security Police Squadron (SPS) assumed security responsibility. A special convoy flight from the 377th SPS was assigned the responsibility to escort this mass weapons movement. A 377th Security Forces crew chief, who worked in the special convoy flight, said, "I really liked it when we convoyed to Kirtland and stopped all the traffic at quitting time."

A 377th security forces TSgt assigned to Manzano tells me, "As the weapons were systematically transferred to the KUMMSC, the structures at Manzano were closed in a phase down of sectors Alpha, Bravo, and Charlie. Because of the dwindling number of weapons, we systematically reduced the security force members manning the base, reflecting the weapon movement to the new WSA. I worked the mountain until the very end in 1992." Manzano was deactivated and designated as "abandoned in place" on October 1, 1992.

In another cost saving move, the Air Force Space Technology Center was combined with three other Air Force laboratories in December 1990, creating the Phillips Laboratory, named after Gen. Samuel C. Phillips, former director of the Apollo Manned Lunar Landing project. The laboratory was operated by the Air Force Material Command, and in 1997, it became part of the larger Air Force Research Laboratory at Kirkland AFB. With the Manzano deactivation, Phillips Laboratory assumed the maintenance responsibility for the former WSA, and Sandia National Laboratories continued to provide security.

Manzano Base was not the only storage site impacted by the weapons de-escalation process. Site Baker at Killeen Base, Texas, was deactivated in 1969, when advances in nuclear technology altered maintenance procedures and storage facilities, and by 1997, several WSAs in the United States, and in foreign locations, either reduced their number of warheads or were closed.

25

Kirtland Underground Munitions Maintenance and Storage Complex

At 34 years old, the maintenance and operational costs for Manzano continued to increase, and with the anticipated closing of other WSAs, it was time to consider a new weapons storage facility. A major assigned to the Air Force Office of Security tells me that in 1980 he was asked to provide an estimate of potential savings if a new WSA was constructed underground. That estimate was a little over $10 million per year which, needless to say, captured the attention of many people.

New Mexico Senator Pete Domenici was a great proponent for nuclear arms and energy development, supporting building the nuclear stockpile and expanding military installations. According to research information, a proposal to create an underground nuclear storage facility at Kirtland AFB was posed to the Senator in 1985. However, at that time he was in negotiations to expand the Los Alamos National Laboratory at Sandia, to accommodate the DoE's interest in developing other energy projects. When the next opportunity presented itself, the storage facility proposal was approved, in great part because of the Senator's leadership and strong insistence. The notice to proceed was given in October 1988.

In November 1988, construction began on the $43 million Kirtland Underground Munitions Maintenance and Storage Complex (KUMMSC), intended to replace Manzano as a WSA. Located three-and one-half miles east of the main base, it is a state-of-the-art facility covering some 56 acres, with more than 300,000 square feet entirely underground, and specifically designed to accommodate the changes in the U.S. nuclear program. With extensive excavation

25. Kirtland Underground Munitions

work completed, contractors started pouring concrete in February 1989 and finished pouring in May 1990. The complex was noted as "substantially complete" in October 1990, just two years from its approval.

The complex was activated in 1992 and operated by the 898th Munitions Squadron, of the 377th Air Base Wing, a unit of the Air Force Global Strike Command, which assumed stewardship as part of the Air Force's efforts to improve the nuclear enterprise. When KUMMSC construction was totally completed in 1994, the transfer of all nuclear warheads from the Manzano WSA facility was also completed.

Air Force Global Strike Command patch (U.S. Air Force, Kirtland AFB).

Although my Freedom of Information Act request asking for certain documents resulted in a letter stating, "The documents are not releasable ... all information is withheld under the government authority to withhold technical data," the existence of KUMMSC, unlike Manzano, has never been in question. The development was not as secretive as was Manzano back in 1946; however, the general public, although aware of the development, knew little about the complex itself. That was until a local television station ran a six-minute news segment about the complex. A book contributor and member of the 377th SPS at Kirtland tells me the TV news reporter had researched the internet and located an Air Force document on file at the Albuquerque public library containing the floor plan of the complex. Feeling the need to make the general public aware, the station created a computer-generated virtual model of the complex based on the floor plan and aired it July 2006. According to a member of the 377th Security Police, the Kirtland Wing Commander about had a meltdown when the video aired and accused the television

Part VI—Miscellaneous Manzano Information

station of endangering national security. The station responded to the commander's fire and fury by proclaiming the video was totally produced from unclassified, public information sources. In the final analysis, nothing happened to the station, but the public was certainly well informed.

In addition to a primary function of testing, maintenance and storage of nuclear weapons, Kirtland acquired the responsibility of dismantling nuclear weapons. As nuclear weapons were returned to the United States from foreign bases, and home bases were selecting weapons for deactivation, many were sent to the Pantex plant in Texas, managed and operated by Consolidated Nuclear Security for the U.S. Department of Energy and Sandia National Laboratories. This plant was originally constructed to produce conventional bombs for the U.S. Army Air Force during the early days of World War II and deactivated when the war ended. The plant was eventually reactivated by the Atomic Energy Commission and since 1975 has been the primary location as a disassembly center for nuclear weapons, doing so at the rate of about seven weapons per day.

Pantex has safely dismantled thousands of weapons retired from the military stockpile and placed the resulting plutonium pits in interim storage. Because of the close proximity to the Pantex plant— and the fact that it already had both a new and an old storage site— Kirtland became important as a trans-shipment base and storage facility, augmenting the Pantex plant.

In 1997, Kirtland became the top nuclear storage area in the United States and has remained so these many years. The number of nuclear weapons stored at the KUMMSC is estimated to be about 2,850, including the ultra-high-yield B83, the most dangerous nuclear weapon in the U.S. arsenal, and several versions of the B61, B61-3, B61-4, B61-7, B61-10, B61-11, and B83. Although not confirmed, the nuclear warheads in storage include the W76, designed for use on the UGM-96 Trident I sea-launched ballistic missiles, the W88 and W87 used on Minuteman III intercontinental ballistic missiles, and the W80-1 designed for use on guided missiles.[1]

The U.S. Air Force currently operates a fleet of 20 B-2A bombers and 46 B-52H bombers capable of delivering a nuclear weapon. Each B-2 can carry up to 16 nuclear weapons, and each B-52H can carry up to 20 air-launched cruise missiles. Research indicates this fleet has approximately 850 nuclear weapons assigned to it, which

25. Kirtland Underground Munitions

includes 528 air-launched cruise missiles. However, only 300 weapons are speculated to be located at bomber bases. The remaining 550 weapons are believed to be maintained in storage at the Kirtland KUMMSC.[2]

In addition to having a highly secured nuclear storage complex, safety was equally a great concern. The 1996 DoD directive 3150.2 established nuclear weapon system safety standards and policy for any location dealing with nuclear weapons, and it is the foundation for all nuclear safety matters. Certification of nuclear weapon facilities and organizations include the successful completion of a Nuclear Weapons Technical Inspection. Each nuclear location receives a periodic safety inspection as mandated by the DoD directive. In January 2010, the 898th Munitions Squadron, which manages and maintains the nuclear warheads in KUMMSC, received a decertification notice based on its previous inspection. This notice meant the squadron could no longer perform its mission of safeguarding the weapons until it passed a follow up nuclear safety inspection. Corrections and changes were made quickly, and the KUMMSC was re-inspected and recertified in June 2010.

Because the secretary of the Air Force considers nuclear deterrence to be the Air Force's first priority, between August and November 2010 the Defense Science Board Permanent Task Force on Nuclear Weapons Surety visited the three major air command headquarters, including the Nuclear Weapons Center at Kirtland AFB. Their report, issued April 2011, indicated that after observing operations and logistics, the Task Force is of the opinion that the Air Force leadership can have high confidence that, with few exceptions, the operating and direct support forces understand their mission and the demands of their mission and are a professional, disciplined and committed force. The processes, discipline, and culture that served the nation well for more than half a century has ensured that the risk of an unauthorized transfer of a nuclear weapon is now near zero and will remain so as long as there is leadership attention and clear direction.[3]

Lt. Gen. Frank Klotz, commander of the Global Strike Command, made the statement, "Our mission is to develop and provide combat-ready forces for nuclear deterrence and global strike operations, safe, secure and credible to support the President of the United Sates and combatant commanders."[4] The formation of Air Force

Part VI—Miscellaneous Manzano Information

Global Strike Command has produced a nearly universally positive response in the nuclear operating forces by developing and implementing a clear set of values:

- Individual responsibility
- Performance self-assessment
- Following directives, without compromise
- Technical and weapons expertise
- Taking pride in the U.S. nuclear heritage program
- Respect for fellow airmen who have proven worthy
- Safety, above all.

Although Kirtland already possessed a superior security system, after the September 11 attack, a decision was made to take no chance on a terrorist attack on the facility. In 2003, a $10 million allocation was approved to install new fencing, new perimeter lighting, and a power system upgrade. An assessment also referenced the need of a concrete barrier at certain areas to prevent a hijacked airliner from crashing through a nuclear weapon storage location.[5]

As strange as it may seem, nuclear weapons continue to be moved by air in and out of KUMMSC through the joint Kirtland and Albuquerque International Airport, as they were in 1955.

26

The 377th Security Forces Squadron

After Manzano merged with Kirtland in 1971, the 4900th Security Police Squadron (SPS) at Kirtland became responsible for Manzano security and remained so until July 1, 1977, when it was inactivated and replaced with the Air Force Systems Command 1606th Air Base Wing. The 1608th Security Police Squadron then acquired security responsibility for Manzano, as nuclear weapons were systematically transferred from the Manzano site to the new Kirtland Underground Munitions and Maintenance Storage Complex (KUMMSC). That transfer was completed in 1992, and the DoD took over Manzano. In 2011, the 377th Security Forces Group was activated to assume the security responsibility. The continuity of responsibility changes is a bit uncertain at this time, but this is the best conclusion I can make.

According to research, the 377th is an old group with a history of sporadic inactivation. As best I can determine, its origin as the 377 Air Police Squadron dates back to April 8, 1966, only to be inactivated May 15, 1967. The 377th Security Police Group was reactivated on June 14, 1985, inactivated in 1991, and reactivated August 2, 2011, as the 377th Security Forces Group (SFG). At present, the SFG consists of two squadrons: the Weapons System Security Squadron (WSSS) and the Security Forces Squadron (SFS).

The SFS provides the day-to-day operations on the main base, including manning the entry gates, and traditional law enforcement activities. Other law enforcement activities around the wing include protocol, dignitary escorts, and traditional investigations handled by OSEI. The SFS also serves as a back-up to the WSSS in defending the weapons storage complex.

The SFS is also responsible for the Pass and Registration activity.

Part VI—Miscellaneous Manzano Information

According to the Kirtland AFB web site, they process and issue DBIDS passes and restricted area badges for nine wings, 110 mission partners, 3,125 members of the military, 1,068 members of the guard and reserve units, 12,000 SNL employees, and approximately 1,000 AF Exchange employees. They process some 200 requests for base access and 60 restricted access badges applications per day, using the National Criminal Information Center Database.[1]

WSSS has the responsibility for the security of the weapons storage complex. The U.S. arsenal of nuclear weapons are stored at an estimated 24 geographical locations in the United States and five countries in Europe. The location with the most nuclear weapons by far is the KUMMSC. Many of the weapons in this location are retired weapons awaiting shipment for dismantlement at the Pantex Plant in Texas, along with 550 nuclear weapons assigned to the strategic bomber groups.

The WSSS is on duty 24/7/365 in the complex, along with a couple of top side mobile units and an overwatch (sniper team). Their responsibility includes the physical protection of materials stored within the complex to mitigate a broad range of threats from theft, diversion, sabotage, espionage, unauthorized access, compromise, and other hostile or noncompliant activities, and they provide security for the complex employees. Security monitoring and protection at the KUMMSC involves alarm management and control, intrusion detection and assessment, access controls, contraband detection, barriers and locks, material accountability, technical surveillance countermeasures, tactical systems, remotely operated weapon systems, countering unmanned aircraft and roving patrols.

In addition to these two squadrons, there is also a 377th Support Flight, which maintains the status of deployed personnel and handles many of the supply functions.

The 377th Security Forces Squadron has a lot of achievements about which to be proud. According to the research information, since its inception, the squadron has received several awards including: Presidential Unit Citation in 1968; the Air Force Outstanding Unit Award with Combat "V" Device in 1971 and 1973; and the Air Force Outstanding Unit Award in 1987 and 1991. The Pass and Registration office was awarded the 2018 SFS Team of the year, the Airman of the 3rd Quarter, NCO of the 1st quarter, 2018 Airman of the year, 2018 NCO of the year, and three Defender of the Month awards.

26. The 377th Security Forces Squadron

The 377th participates in many base activities each year to recognize special events. One such event is Police Week at Kirtland. On May 15, 1962, a proclamation was signed by President John Kennedy designating that day Peace Officers Memorial Day, and the week surrounding that date as Police Week. This annual event at Kirtland recognizes the security forces heritage and honors those who have served therein. Police Week permits the opportunity for the SFG, other base personnel, and the community to interact through events such as a softball tournament, a golf tournament, a resiliency briefing and a community outreach day. The Air Force Security Forces Association Chapter in Albuquerque was recognized in 2021 by the Wing Commander for the great support they always provide.

The Heritage Room

The 377th has a special way to recognize its long history through its Heritage Room. The room, originally identified as the SFS Heritage Room, was established back in 1966 and was used primarily to conduct guard mounts and training. It was repurposed in 2008 as a meeting room and a way to remember and honor those in the 377th. It is filled with donated memorabilia, historical pieces, photographs and a photographic timeline, which tells the story of those who served in Tan Son Nhut Air Field, South Vietnam, Ramstein AB in Germany, and Kirtland AFB. Another addition to the room is the original Klaxon security alert alarm from the old Manzano barracks.

Airmen assigned to the 377th Special Forces Group have an opportunity to see the legacy of the unit which they will be a part of and reflect on the prior missions undertaken by the 377th Air Police, Security Police and Security Forces squadrons. It is a place where stories and experiences are shared with others to relive old memories and appreciate friendships. The room is managed by the Albuquerque chapter of the Security Forces Association. Chief Master Sgt. Brady L. McCoy, SFG chief enlisted manager, states: "Our story in the 377 SFG will now endure for many, many years to come."[2]

As with all security forces squadrons, it is important to be physically fit and mentally alert to maintain the readiness response necessary for any security incident. To help accomplish these objectives, training is a consistent activity for members of the SFG. Several

Part VI—Miscellaneous Manzano Information

The 377th Heritage Room (A1C Ireland Summers, Kirtland AFB Public Affairs).

The 377th Heritage Room (A1C Ireland Summers, Kirtland AFB Public Affairs).

26. The 377th Security Forces Squadron

of these activities occur annually such as the Manzano Challenge, which began in October 2016, the Force-on-Force training, and the Active Shooter event. These training events are ways to test members in different tactical scenarios and prepare them to function and survive in different situations. Activities include weapons skills, land navigation, problem solving, team work and tactics and learning to overcome obstacles and demonstrate skills proficiency. Awards include a trophy and a year's bragging rights.

In his address to the Senate Armed Services Committee on May 1, 2019, Gen. Timothy M. Ray, commander, Air Force Global Strike Command made the statement, "Security is one of the most fundamental competencies the nation demands of the military.... This involves more than Security Forces at the gate; this is preparing for cyberwarfare, threats involving unmanned aerial systems, and other potential threats across multiple domains ... progress is being made to shape the future of Security Forces as an elite, integrated team prepared to face the threats they encounter in and around our installations and missile fields."[3]

The 377th SFG continues to develop technology and strategy to defend against these threats by taking Security Forces training and operations in a more relevant and realistic direction.

27

Manzano Today

Since its closing in 1992, Manzano WSA continues to be used by several groups for many different purposes. After the closing, Phillips Laboratory assumed responsibility for Manzano's on-going maintenance, and a former Sandia National Laboratories (SNL) security manager and book contributor tells me that SNL assumed the primary security responsibility for Manzano, including the access gate, perimeter patrols and alarm system. He says the 377th SF teams at Kirtland provides support to the SNL security team as needed. Over the years, the SNL continued to develop their tech areas and added a number of facilities in the area known as Coyote Test Field, adjacent to Manzano.

The DoE-leased facilities at Manzano for SNL to store low-level radioactive waste, mixed waste, and transuranic waste were given consideration as a nuclear pit storage facility. As discussed in Chapter Thirteen, the pit or capsule is the spherical mass of plutonium, roughly the size of a grapefruit, which is the fission core that triggers a nuclear weapon explosion. The Texas Pantex Plant continued the life-preserving assembly and disassembly operations and related activities of environmental protection, restoration and transportation of pit components. In March 1996, as a plant upgrade to meet waste operational efficiency and safety regulatory requirements was contemplated, the DoE also conducted an environmental impact analysis of the Pantex Plant, giving consideration to the feasibility of relocating some or all pit storage to another site.

Manzano met all of the required criteria for a storage facility, and the Nuclear Weapons Council Staff considered it one of 60 viable locations. The 41structures tunneled into the mountain created a very safe and convenient place to store pits. A visit to Manzano indicated (1) no major modifications were required to the structures, (2) a breach of storage containers resulting from an aircraft crash would

27. Manzano Today

not result in a release of radioactive gases or particles because of the type of structure construction, and (3) pit storage activities would have no negative impact on any historic cultural resources. Meeting the selection criteria validating its suitability, Manzano was confirmed to be a prime alternative location for storing up to 20,000 pits.[1] The USAF concurred that Manzano possessed sufficient storage and capacity and could be made available for immediate use, and it consented to be a cooperating agency. However, the conclusion of the impact analysis, published in March 1997, was to upgrade the facilities at the Pantex plant through new construction providing for continued pit storage and to increase the storage level from 12,000 to 20,000 pits.

The United States ceased production of nuclear pits in large numbers in 1989, when the Rocky Flats Plant near Denver was closed because of environmental violations, leaving the United States without an industrial-scale manufacturing capacity. At the time of closing, the Rocky Flats Plant was manufacturing some 1,000 pits per year, and since the closing, only 30 weapon pits have been fabricated, all at the Los Alamos National Laboratory (LANL). Currently, the United States has about 20,000 pits, and of those, some 12,000 are inside nuclear warheads or ready to be placed in one. In 2008, the new administrator of the National Nuclear Security Administration (NNSA), addressing a Congressional hearing, stated that she intended to make pit production the number one priority in modernizing the NNSA infrastructure. Finally, in May 2018, the NNSA publicized that the Nuclear Weapons Council had approved its plan to produce a minimum of 80 pits per year, and that decision was re-confirmed in January 2020. Pit production will occur at the Savannah River Site in South Carolina, and the LANL facilities.[2] Although possible, I have found nothing to confirm or deny pit storage at Manzano.

According to a Sandia National Laboratories-New Mexico Facilities and Safety Information Document, Manzano bunkers numbers 37055, 37057, 37063, and 37078 were being used to store nuclear material, radioactive material, spent fuel, sealed sources, chemicals, explosives, and other hazardous material. Even after the weapons were transferred to the KUMMSC, the Defense Nuclear Facilities Safety Board (DNFSB) continued to include Manzano in its inspection and safety oversight procedures because it remained

Part VI—Miscellaneous Manzano Information

in a nuclear waste classification status. An inspection was conducted in June 1994 for the DoE leased storage bunkers and cited for several violations. Among those violations were: (1) failure to maintain a logbook of critical material stored in each bunker and posted in a conspicuous place near the bunker, (2) maintaining fire hazard material (e.g., wood pallets and crates) too close to the bunkers, and (3) failing to indicate the type or category of material, amount, degree of enrichment and radiation level on the exterior of the storage vessel.[3]

Because of the associated oversight support required, there was a desire to reduce the nuclear footprint and consolidate nuclear material throughout the DoE. The SNL waste management department operated two Hazard Category 3 (HC-3) nuclear waste facilities, one located at Manzano and the other an HC-3 Transportation unit. A concerted effort began in early 2014 to downgrade these two facilities from a nuclear waste status to a non-nuclear status. The requirements, completed in March 2014, retired the nuclear operations at Manzano and the HC-3 Transportation unit. Safety oversight was transferred from the DNFSB to the Industrial Facility Safety Basis. The SNL has also used a few of the underground bunkers for nuclear testing.[4]

In addition to nuclear related storage, other items such as furniture, document boxes, and classified information were stored in several bunkers. These are items that can easily be removed and the space made available for other activity, if needed. Information in the 2017 SNL Nuclear Material Initiatives/Successes meeting, May 15, 2017, indicated that some 750 classified items had been removed from Manzano bunkers. Of those items, 100 were permanently disposed of offsite, and three bunkers of storage space were reclaimed. The report also noted that the process of bunker consolidation, removing stored material from the Manzano bunkers, continued as an on-going project.[5]

In late 1991, the DoE expanded its Central Training Academy and started using the vacated buildings at Manzano as classrooms. Wackenhut Services, Inc., was the contractor hired for this training, and employed several retired AF security personnel who were stationed at Manzano. A retired AF colonel and book contributor, who became the deputy general manager for Wackenhut Services, Inc., told me, "We used all the old Manzano buildings as well

27. Manzano Today

as the shooting range complex to conduct over 150 training courses either on campus, by correspondence or by mobile training teams. We engineered and developed the first Distance Learning training program through a live television feed to DoE sites, using a satellite transmission. A first for the 1990s."

Another book contributor, a retired AF lieutenant colonel and the first manager of the DoE's Information Security Training Department, 1991 through 1996, said, "I was hired by Wackenhut Services Inc. to manage the DoE's training program for protective force personnel, e.g., contractor guards at various DoE facilities. Those training courses included: Information Security, Materials Controls Leadership, Management and Firearms skills. The DoE continues to do safeguards and security training at Manzano to this day. They are now referred to as the National Training Center."

Manzano may be considered a relic of the past, but even today its rich history continues to influence the future of our nuclear weapon program. For example, in May 2019, researchers from the Lawrence Livermore National Laboratory (LLNL) in California combed through the remaining wreckage of the B-29, locating several small fragments of the high explosives from the MK 4 bomb the plane was carrying. In January 2020, the fragments were collected by the Kirtland AFB 377th Air Base Wing Explosive Ordnance Disposal and shipped to LLNL for a thorough evaluation. Of great interest was how exposure to the elements influenced the aging process and changed the chemical, physical, and dimensional properties of the bomb material. One researcher said, "These naturally aged samples could provide a way to validate their assumptions about understanding how high explosives age, and how degradation might impact safety and performance is of critical importance to national security." The information from these fragments also provides valuable insight into the life extension program's annual evaluation of the current nuclear weapon stockpile.[6]

According to information provided by SNL management, the Manzano MSA is a registered Historic District, and 27 historic and prehistoric archaeological sites have been found in the WSA. Of these sites, eight have been recommended for inclusion in the National Register of Historic Places and 14 others are considered to be potentially eligible for inclusion. The B-29 crash site is the most nationally significant site on the WSA because of its association with

Part VI—Miscellaneous Manzano Information

early Cold War weapons program. Work continues to restore the degrading infrastructure of the base.

In many ways, Manzano continues to have the same intrigue it possessed during its active years. I made an inquiry to the Sandia National Laboratories as to the current use of the site, the budget allocations, number of employees, and future plans for the site. I received a reply from the Media Relations Department that the information about Manzano "was not in their purview." So, the mystery and mystique continue 74 years after construction started.

At one point in time we who were stationed there had a significant amount of knowledge about the base, as outsiders pondered, "What was going on behind those fences?" Now those of us who were once stationed there have joined that outsiders' group as we speculate, "Now what is really going on behind those fences?"

Epilogue

Being stationed at Manzano was a unique experience for most of us. In many ways, the duty was different from a traditional Air Force base, as were the memories we carried with us when we left. Chief Si'ahl, also known as Chief Seattle of the Duwamish Tribe, a nature lover and environmentalist, once said, "Take only memories, leave only footprints."[1] I think that is exactly what we did. We left many footprints on Manzano soil and took many memories with us when we left. Writing and compiling this book, I realized that Manzano had made me stronger in history appreciation, blessed by memories of people and events, and refreshed by the personal stories of book contributors. It has been a great walk down memory lane. An 84-year-old book contributor said, "You're really presenting a challenge, but I can still remember those times at Manzano. In some ways, I have fond memories, and some, not so good." Another contributor, 85 years old, stated, "You certainly brought back many unforgettable and super memories." Several contributors and former personnel stationed at Manzano share his sentiment.

As I researched material for this book I came across a jacket patch, created by an unidentified person, which I purchased and proudly display with my USAF memorabilia. The patch adequately

A Manzano jacket patch.

Epilogue

conveys the thoughts for many of the thousands of personnel who were stationed at Manzano over the years, and I know of no better way to close the book than to include a copy, and let it speak for all of us.

Appendix A:
Aerial View of Manzano Base
(Kirtland AFB)

This aerial view (facing page) provides a good perspective of the size of Manzano WSA. The administrative area is located in the lower-left corner of the photo in the shape of a half-hexagon, and the entry control point into the "Q" area is at the south end of that half hexagon. The perimeter road with the three security fences around the base is approximately 10 miles in length. The internal roads comprise some 70 miles connecting bunkers, plants, and storage facilities. Several nuclear weapons storage bunkers are easily defined on these roads on both the east and west sides of the mountain.

Aerial View of Manzano Base (Kirtland AFB)

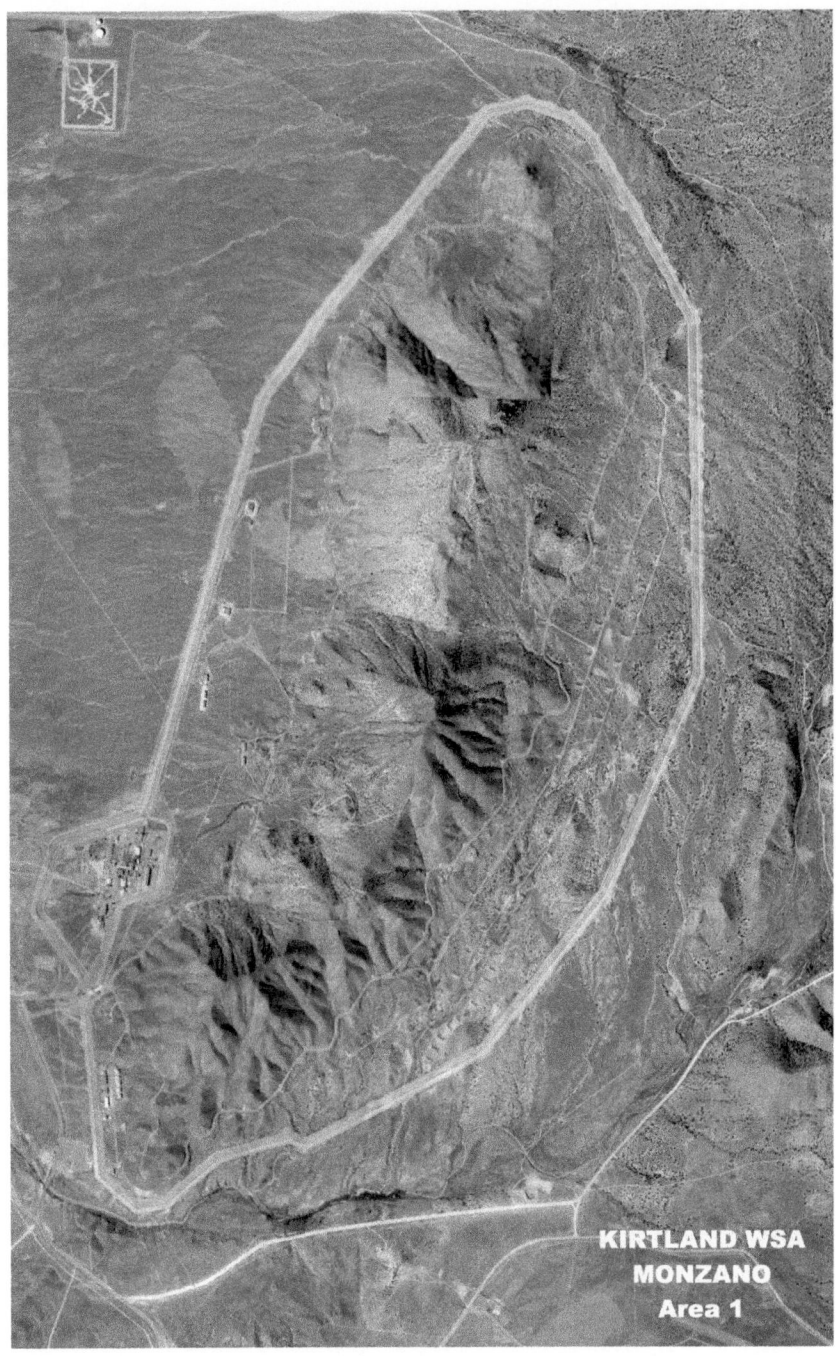

Appendix B: Wall Map Displayed in the ADT Monitoring Room

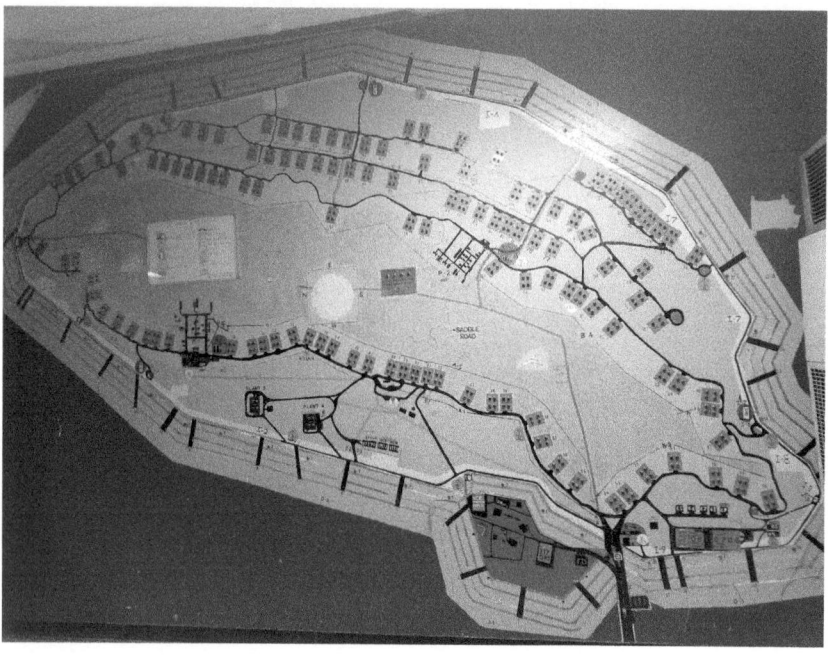

Wall map displayed in the ADT Monitoring Room (private collection).

This map, located in the CSC/ADT control room, is a visual display of the administrative area, the "Q" area, internal roads, storage bunkers, plants, and storage buildings. As discussed in Chapter 18, the map contained three lights (green, amber, red) for each structure, plant, and perimeter fence section reflecting its security status. A quick glance at this map identifies the current status of each facility, and any potential security breach location. The map also indicates the locations of the three aircraft crashes referenced in Chapter 21.

Appendix C: Abbreviated Chronological History of Manzano

1945

After the end of World War II, the Manhattan Project Z Division, working at the Los Alamos laboratory, relocated to the old Oxnard field, which became known as Sandia Base. With the continued production of nuclear weapons, storage sites were necessary. Six possible National Stockpile sites were identified, and the first location selected, identified as "Site Able," was in the Manzano Mountains in Albuquerque, New Mexico.

1946

With the feasibility study completed and the project approved, the Albuquerque District of the U.S. Army Corps of Engineers was granted $10 million to build "Site Able."

1947

Nuclear weapons became a major focus with the establishment of the Air Force, the CIA, and the NSA.

Construction at Site Able started June 1947 under the top-secret project designated "Operation Water Supply." The Armed Forces Special Weapons Project (AFSWP) was created to assume all military functions of the Manhattan Engineering District and assumed responsibility for the Sandia based Z Division.

Appendix C

1949

In addition to storage structures, weapons maintenance plants I and II were tunneled deep into the mountain. These plants were designed for assembly and maintenance of the Mark 5 and Mark 6, first-generation atomic, conventional "Fat Man" type of weapons. Plant I, located on the west face of the mountain, became operational.

1950

Site Able Weapons Storage Area (WSA) became operational April 4, 1950, under the oversight of the Army's 8460th Special Weapons Group. Weapons Maintenance Plant II, located on the east face of the mountain, was completed.

1952

On February 22, 1952, Site Able was renamed Manzano Base WSA. Operational control was turned over to the Air Force and the 1094th Special Reporting Group was created to manage the base. Manzano was a self-contained installation but relied on Sandia Base for logistical support.

1953

Construction started on a new free-standing weapons maintenance plant, designated as number III, designed to service thermonuclear weapons.

1954

As production of thermonuclear weapons continued to increase, 1954 presented the need to add an additional weapons maintenance plant. Designated as plant IV, another free-standing plant, also devoted to thermonuclear weapons.

1955

In June, the 1094 Special Reporting Group became the 1094th Aviation Depot Group with three support squadrons. Construction on weapons maintenance plant number IV was completed.

Abbreviated Chronological History of Manzano

1959

The AFSWP was reorganized and designated the Defense Atomic Support Agency (DASA) and Sandia Base became DASA Headquarters Field Office Command. Manzano came under DASA oversight.

1961

Manzano WSA construction was determined to be totally completed with a total of 122 storage structures (bunkers/ igloos/ magazines) built. Forty-one structures were tunneled into the mountain, and 81 were free-standing structures.

1970

As part of a budget efficiency initiative, President Richard Nixon signed an executive order creating a committee to investigate the possibility of consolidating the three Albuquerque bases, Sandia, Manzano, and Kirtland AFB, into one base.

1971

Deputy Secretary of Defense David Packard announced in March the decision to merge Sandia and Manzano into Kirtland AFB and place it under the Air Force Systems Command. The merger was concurrent with the change of the Defense Atomic Support Agency into the Defense Nuclear Agency. On July 1, 1971, the 3098th Aviation Depot Squadron was activated to replace the 1094th Aviation Depot Group. Manzano Base and Sandia Base were officially merged into Kirtland Air Force Base.

After the merger was completed, routine service and maintenance work performed on weapons at the four Manzano plants were consolidated into plants III and IV. Plant number I was utilized as a communications center for the security police, and Plant number II was used as storage space for various nuclear components and other equipment.

Appendix C

1977

Military Airlift Command took control of Kirtland, and the 1606th Air Base Wing took over as host unit. The 1608th Security Police Squadron became responsible for Manzano security.

1988

Construction started in November on a new $43 million Kirtland Underground Munitions Maintenance and Storage Complex (KUMMSC) to replace Manzano WSA.

1990

Construction at the KUMMSC was considered substantially complete in October.

1991

The process to transfer nuclear weapons to KUMMSC began. A special 377th Security Police Squadron convoy flight at Kirtland was assigned the responsibility to escort the convoys transferring the weapons to the KUMMSC. The DoE expanded its Central Training Academy and started using the vacated buildings at Manzano as classrooms. Wackenhut Services, Inc., was the contractor hired for this training and employed several retired AF security personnel who were stationed at Manzano.

1992

The KUMMSC was officially activated, operated by the 898th Munitions Squadron and the 377th Weapons Systems Security Squadron. The 377th Security Police Squadron provided security for Manzano until it closed. Manzano WSA was officially closed in June, and Phillips Laboratory assumed responsibility for its maintenance. Sandia National Laboratories continued to provide security for the base because some of the old Manzano bunkers were used as storage for SNL nuclear components and miscellaneous merchandise.

Abbreviated Chronological History of Manzano

1993

On January 1, 1993, command of Kirtland AFB was transferred from the Air Mobility Command to the newly formed Air Force Material Command, and the 377th Air Base Wing was reactivated to become the base's host organization.

1994

The KUMMSC construction was completed, as was the transfer of nuclear weapons from the Manzano.

On the first of April 1994, the 898th Munitions Squadron was established, assuming the responsibility for the Kirtland WSA.

1997

Kirtland KUMMSC became the top nuclear storage area in the United States and has remained the top storage area.

2008

In 2008, the Manzano was a candidate as a pit/capsule storage facility. The 41 structures tunneled into the mountain provided a very safe place to store up to 20,000 pits.

2011

The 377th Security Forces Group and the 377th Weapons Systems Security Squadron were activated at Kirtland.

2015

The 377th Air Base Wing was reassigned from Air Force Materiel Command to Air Force Global Strike Command.

2017

The Manzano Storage Consolidation Project continued as part of the Sandia National Laboratories Nuclear Material Initiative. Classified items continued to be moved from Manzano structures and permanently disposed of offsite, and storage space was reclaimed.

Appendix D: Manzano Base Commanders

I have been unable to locate a published list of Manzano base commanders. The list below is comprised of a few names found during research and several names provided by book contributors, representing their best recollections. My apologies for any errors, any misspellings, and the incompleteness of names. Eventually, a complete and accurate list will be compiled, perhaps from this start.

U.S. Army, 8460th Special Weapons Group—1947–1952
Col. Gilbert Dorland, circa 1950–1952
Col. R. Potter Campbell, Jr., Executive Officer

**United States Air Force,
1094th Special Reporting Group—1952–1971**
Col. Jack Armstrong, circa 1952–1954
Col. Ralph I. Williams, circa 1954–1956
Col Childers, circa 1955
Col. Benjamin Whitsell, circa 1959–1963
Col. Raymond M. Hubbard, circa 1964–1966
Col. Timlin, circa 1968
Col. Jack Hughes (dates unknown)

Manzano Merged into Kirtland 1971
Col. Charles G. Mathison, Kirtland Base Commander
Oct 1970–1972

Appendix E: Department of the Air Force Letter

HEADQUARTERS 377TH AR AASE WING (AFMC)

30 Dec 02

Memorandum FOR 377 ABW/IG

FROM: 377 ABW/PAC, Mitch Chandran

SUBJECT: Congressional Inquiry—KVA02-291

In accordance with Air Force Instruction 35-101, paragraph 7.22, I can neither confirm nor deny the presence of nuclear weapons or radioactive nuclear weapon components on Kirtland Air Force Base.

Mitchell B. Chandran. Civilian
NflTC1-ELL B. CHANDRAN, USAF

Appendix F: Frequently Used Abbreviations and Acronyms

AAC	Army Air Corp.
ADT	American District Telegraph Co. (electronic security and alarm monitoring services)
AF	Air Force
AP	Air Police
AFB	Air Force Base
AFSC	Air Force Specialty Code
AFSWP	Armed Forces Special Weapons Project
A1C	Airman First Class
A2C	Airman Second Class
Capt.	Captain
Col.	Colonel
CSC	Central Security Control
DASA	Defense Atomic Support Agency
DoD	Department of Defense
DoE	Department of Energy
DNA	Defense Nuclear Agency
KAFB	Kirtland Air Force Base
KUMMSC	Kirtland Underground Munitions Maintenance and Storage Complex
Lt.	Lieutenant

Frequently Used Abbreviations and Acronyms

Lt Col.	Lieutenant Colonel
MK	Mark, an identifier for a type nuclear weapon
MSgt	Master Sergeant
NNSA	National Nuclear Security Administration
NCOIC	Non-Commissioned Officer in Charge
OIC	Officer in Charge
Q Area	The restricted access secured area, requiring a high-level security clearance
Q Gate	The access gate to enter or depart the restricted area
SF	Security Force
SFS	Security Forces Squadron
SNL	Sandia National Laboratories
SPS	Security Police Squadron
SSgt.	Staff Sergeant
TSgt	Technical Sergeant
USAF	United States Air Force
WSA	Weapons Storage Area
WSS	Weapons Storage Site

Chapter Notes

Epigraph

1. Kenney, Douglas L., 15 Minutes: General Curtis LeMay and the Countdown to Nuclear Annihilation (St. Martin's Press, 2011).
2. Inaugural Address of President John F. Kennedy, John F. Kennedy Presidential Library, January 20, 1961, www.jfklibrary.org.

Preface

1. Chandran, Mitchell B., USAF, Memorandum for 377 ABW/IG, December 30, 2002.

Chapter 1

1. Bartimus, Tad, and Scott McCartney, *Trinity's Children: Living Along America's Nuclear Highway* (Harcourt, 1992).
2. Albuquerque History, www.albuquerqueinfonetwork.com/albuquerque.
3. Wikipedia Encyclopedia, www.wikipedia.com.
4. Albuquerque Historical Society, www.albuqhistoc.org.
5. United States Census Bureau, www.census.gov.
6. Brunt, Charles D., "Rising on the Mesa," *Albuquerque Journal*, April 9, 2016.
7. Kirtland AFB History, www.kirtland.af.mil.
8. Kirtland AFB History, www.kirtland.af.mil.
9. Bartlett, Nancy, "Interviews Tell of NM Bataan Death March Survivors," *Albuquerque Journal*, August 1, 2020.
10. Biggers, Ashley, "The Spy House, Secret Albuquerque," YouTube, January 2020.
11. Cohen, Kelly, "Los Alamos Worker Sentenced for Trying to Pass U.S. Nuclear Secrets to Venezuela," *Washington Examiner*, August 23, 2014, www.washingtonexaminer.com.

Chapter 2

1. Albuquerque History, www.albuquerqueinfonetwork.com/albuquerque.
2. Manzano Mountains State Park, New Mexico Bureau of Geology and Mineral Resources, https://geoinfo.nmt.edu/tour/state.
3. Weiser, Kathy, Legends of America, More New Mexico Treasures, Tijeris Canyon, February 2020, www.legendsofamerica.com/mor.
4. Kenney, Douglas L., *15 Minutes: General Curtis LeMay and the Countdown to Nuclear Annihilation* (St. Martin's Press, 2011).
5. Strauss, Lewis L., "Development of the Thermonuclear Bomb," Nuclearfiles.org/library/correspondence/Strauss, November 1949.
6. "The History of Nuclear Energy," U.S. Department of Energy, albert-cordova.com/ans/DOE/NE0088.
7. Loeber, Charles R., "Building the Bombs," Sandia National Laboratories, 2002, www.sandia.gov/about/history.
8. Wikipedia Encyclopedia, www.wikipedia.com.
9. General Groves comments when the AEC took over the Manhattan

192

Chapter Notes

project, *Oak Ridge Journal*, January 2, 1947, www.y.12.doe.gov/sites.

10. Kenney, Douglas L., *15 Minutes: General Curtis LeMay and the Countdown to Nuclear Annihilation* (St. Martin's Press, 2011).

11. Atomic Energy Act, Section 10 (b) Restrictions (5) (B) (b) (iv), 1946.

12. Goodwin, Christopher R., and associates, "Air Force Ammunition and Explosive Storage & Unaccompanied Personnel Housing During the Cold War (1946–1989)," August 2008, https://archive.org/details/kirtlandafb.

Chapter 3

1. Loeber, Charles R., "Building the Bombs."

2. Sandia National Laboratories, 2002, www.sandia.gov/about/history.

3. Wikipedia Encyclopedia, Sandia Base, www.wikipedia.com.

4. Robinson, Paul, "Radiation Releases at Sandia National Laboratories/New Mexico, Final Report," March 2006, www.sric.org/nuclear/docs/robinson.

5. Wolf, Amy F., "The U.S. Nuclear Weapons Complex: Overview of Department of Energy Sites," Congressional Research Service, February 2020, https://srsreports.congress.gov.

6. Robinson, Paul, "Radiation Releases at Sandia National Laboratories/New Mexico, Final Report," March 2006.

7. "What Became of Sandia Base?" www.answers.com, November 11, 2009.

8. Wolf, Amy F., "The U.S. Nuclear Weapons Complex: Overview of Department of Energy Sites," Congressional Research Service, February 2020, https://srsreports.congress.gov.

Chapter 4

1. Page, Joseph T., "Bombs Away: A Brief 75th Anniversary History of Kirtland Air Force Base, New Mexico," October 2016.

2. Kirtland Air Force Base, Colonel Roy C. Kirtland, March 27, 2013, wwwkirtland.af.mil/about us/facts sheet.

3. Kirtland, National Archives, https://catalog.archives.gov/id/10457039.

4. Ray, Timothy M., General, Commander Air Force Global Strike Force, presentation to the Senate Armed Service Committee, Subcommittee on Strategic Forces, May 1, 2019.

Chapter 5

1. First History of AFSWP, 1947–1948, National Technical Information Services, U.S. Department of Commerce, https://ntrl.ntis.gov.

2. Welsh, Michael, "A Mission in the Desert: Albuquerque District U.S. Corp of Engineers History."

3. Goodwin, Christopher, and associates, "Air Force Ammunition and Explosive Storage & Unaccompanied Personnel Housing During the Cold War (1946–1989)."

4. Sandia Base/Manzano Base, www.liquisearch.com.

5. Norris, Robert S., and Hans M. Kristensen, "Global Nuclear Weapons Inventories, 1954–2010," https://doi.org/10.2968/066004008 (used as the reference for nuclear weapons inventories in the book).

6. Weitze, Karen J., *Keeping the Edge: Air Force Material Command Cold War Context (1945–1991), Volume II Installations and Facilities* (Headquarters, Air Force Materiel Command, 2003).

Chapter 6

1. Abrahamson, James, "The Sandia Pioneers," *American Diplomacy*, June 2002, https://americandiplomacy.web.unc.edu/2002/06/thesandiapioneers.

2. The Army Historical Foundation, https://armyhistory.org/8460thspecialweaponsgroup.

3. First History of AFSWP, 1947–1948.

4. Wikipedia Encyclopedia, Operation Sandstone, https://en.wikipedia.org/wiki/operationsandstone.

5. Norris, Robert S., and Hans M. Kristensen, "Global Nuclear Weapons Inventories, 1954–2010."

Chapter Notes

6. Dase, Amy E., and Stephanie L. Katauskas, "For Love of Country: the Killeen Base Oral History Project," September 2011, www.nicap.org/docs/54 1001killeen.

Chapter 8

1. Manzano Base, Albuquerque, New Mexico, welcome booklet, information services office.
2. First History of AFSWP, 1947–1948.

Chapter 9

1. DoD Directive Number 5210.41, Criteria and Standards for Safeguarding Atomic Weapons, 8 December 1962.
2. Loeber, Charles R., "Building the Bombs," Sandia National Laboratories, 2002.
3. Wikipedia Encyclopedia, https://en.wikipedia.org/wiki/twomanrule.

Chapter 10

1. Wikipedia Encyclopedia, George F. Kennan, www.wikipedia.com.
2. Central Intelligence Agency, The Effect of the Soviet Possibility of Atomic Bombs on the Security of the United States, June 9, 1950, www.alternatewars.com/ww3/ww3/documents/CIA.
3. Norris, Robert S. and Hans M. Kristensen, "Global Nuclear Weapons Inventories, 1954–2010."
4. Higgins, Richard, "New Mexico: Atomic Spy Capital," Warfare History Network www.warfarehistory.com.
5. Nuclear Weapons: Mark 5, Mark 6, Mark 17, and Mark 24, Wikipedia Encyclopedia—Nuclear Bombs, www.wikipedia.org.
6. Clancy, Tom, *The Sum of All Fears* (G.P. Putnam's Sons, 1991).
7. *Sum of All Fears*, Paramount Pictures, 5555 Melrose Avenue, Hollywood, CA, 90038, 2002.
8. Woke, Herman S, "Making the H-Bomb," *Air Force Magazine*, March 2009, www.airforcemag.com/article/H_bomb.
9. U.S. Enduring Nuclear Weapon Stockpile, August 2007, www.nuclearweaponsarchive.org
10. Stockholm International Peace Research Institute, June 2021, Zeenews, https://zeenews.india.com/world.

Chapter 11

1. Goodwin, Christopher, and associates, "Air Force Ammunition and Explosive Storage & Unaccompanied Personnel Housing During the Cold War (1946–1989)."
2. Global Security, Weapons of Mass Destruction, Manzano, www.globalsecurity.org/wmd/facility/manzano.
3. Goodwin, R. Christopher, and associates, "Air Force Ammunition and Explosive Storage & Unaccompanied Personnel Housing During the Cold War (1946–1989)" (note: all structure details extracted from this report).
4. Goodwin and associates, Type B structure, p. 23.
5. Goodwin and associates, Type C structure, p. 27.
6. Goodwin and associates, Type D structure, p. 23.
7. Goodwin and associates, Type A Structures, p. 20.
8. Goodwin and associates, Type S Structure, p. 26.
9. Norris, Robert S., and Hans M. Kristensen, "Global Nuclear Weapons Inventories, 1954–2010."
10. Weapons Storage and Security System (WS3), Wikipedia Encyclopedia, https://en.wikipedia.org/wiki/weapons.

Chapter 12

1. Department of Defense manual, Nuclear Weapons Personnel Reliability Program, January 2015, www.esd.whs.mil/portals/54.
2. Goodwin, R. Christopher, and associates, "Air Force Ammunition and Explosive Storage & Unaccompanied Personnel Housing During the Cold War (1946–1989)" (note: all plant details extracted from this report).

Chapter Notes

3. Goodwin, R. Christopher, and associates, plant numbers, I and II, p. 20, 25.
4. Goodwin, R. Christopher, and associates, plant number III, p. 25.
5. Goodwin, R. Christopher, and associates, plant number IV, p. 26.
6. Kenney, Douglas, L., *15 Minutes*, p. 155.
7. Kenney, Douglas, L., *15 Minutes*, p. 3.
8. Wikipedia Encyclopedia, Castle Bravo, www.wikipedia.com.
9. Global Security, Weapons of Mass Destruction, Manzano, www.globalsecurity.org/wmd/facility/manzano.

Chapter 13

1. Goodwin, R. Christopher, and associates, pits, p. 19.
2. Wolf, Amy F., "The Nuclear Weapons Complex: Overview of Department of Energy Sites, Congressional Research Service," February 2020, https://srsreports.congress.gov.
3. Nuclear Watch, "NNSA Releases Draft Environmental Assessment," February 2018, www. nukewatch.org/press release.
4. Nuclear Watch, South Carolina Environmental Law Project, June 2021, https://nukewatch.org/issues/plutonium-pitproduction.

Chapter 15

1. The Free Library by Farlex, The Marechaussee Corps., www.the freelibrary.com/themarechaussee.
2. United States Air Force Security Forces, Military Police (Aviation) and Air Base Defender Battalions, https://en.wikipedia.org/wiki/united_states_air_force_security_forces.
3. Wheeler, Derrick, A1C,1608th SPS, "History of Manzano Weapons Storage Area," date unknown.
4. First History of AFSWP, 1947–1948.

Chapter 16

1. "Teenager Dies at Nuclear Site," *The Delta Democrat-Times*, Greenville, MS, May 28, 1972

Chapter 17

1. USAF Nuclear Surety Tamper Control and Detection Programs, AF Instruction 91–104, April 2013, https://fas.org/irp.

Chapter 19

1. Casadel, Greg, *A Gun and Cherries in a Bucket of Blood* (Xlibris, 2014).

Chapter 20

1. Nofil, Brianna, History Stories—Transportation—White Trains, May 2018, www.history.com/nuclea.
2. Office of Secure Transportation, U.S. Department of Energy, Wikipedia Encyclopedia, www.wikipedia.com.

Chapter 21

1. Albuquerque International Sunport, Facts and Figures, www.abqsunport.com/facts-figures.
2. Aviation Safety Network, B-29 Superfortress Crash, Manzano Base, https://avation-safety.net/98583.
3. Demerly, Tom, "The Variationist, This Day in 1957: Biggest Bomber, Biggest H-Bomb, and Biggest Near Catastrophe in History," May 22, 2020, www.theaviationist.com.
4. Declassified F-100 Crash Report, purchased from the Aviation Archaeological Investigation and Research.
5. Martin/General Dynamics RB-57-CF, 1963 USAF Serial Numbers, www.joebaugher.com/usafserialnumber-1963.
6. Beitler, Stu, "Manzano Base, NM Tactical Air Command Jet Crashes September 1977," www.disaaters.com/new mexico, and Aviation Safety Network, https://aviation-safety.net/database/recoird/php197709140.
7. Hickman, Kennedy, "The Raid on

Chapter Notes

Son Tay, Vietnam War Operation to Save POW's," www.thoughtcompany.com/Vietnam_War.

Chapter 23

1. Wikipedia Encyclopedia, Project Blue Book www.wikipedia.com/wiki/project_blue_book.
2. Lawhon, Loy, "Kirtland AFB Sightings," https://www.ufoevidence.org/cases.
3. UFO Alien Database, https://ufo.fandom.com/wiki/manzano_base.
4. Barkun, Michael, *A Culture of Conspiracy: Apocalyptic Visions in Contemporary America* (University of California Press, 2006).
5. Wikipedia Encyclopedia, "Kirtland AFB UFO Sighting," www.wikipedia.com/wiki/kirtland.
6. Kirtland AFB UFO landing, https://www.thinkaboutitdocs.com/Kirtland, Air Force Base/1980.
7. Hastings, Robert, "UFO's and Nukes," www.ufohastings.com.
8. Goodwin, Christopher, and associates, p. 15.

Chapter 24

1. "How Many Nukes and Where Are They," National Electronic Briefing Book No. 97, nsarchives2.gwu.edu.
2. Permissive Action Link, Wikipedia Encyclopedia, www.en.wikipedia.org/wiki/permissive.
3. Deaver, Michael, K., *A Different Drummer: My Thirty Years with Ronald Reagan* (HarperCollins, 2010).
4. Arm Control Treaties, www.atomicarchive.com/resources/treaties.
5. "How Many Nukes and Where Are They," National Electronic Briefing Book No. 97, nsarchives2.gwu.edu.
6. NSC 68: United States Objectives and Programs for National Security, www.citizensource.com/history/20thcen.
7. Transcript of President Dwight D. Eisenhower's Farewell Address (1961), www.ourdocuments.gov.
8. Records of the Defense Nuclear Agency, 374.2 General Records of the AFSWP, www.national archives.gov/research.
9. U.S. Air Force, Air Force Material Command, August 2015, www.af.mil/aboutus/facts.
10. Meeting on merge of Kirtland-Sandia-Manzano Bases, 13 May 1971, internal, unpublished document provided by the Kirtland AFB historian.
11. Van Citters, Karen, and Kristen Bisson, "Historic Context and Evaluation for Kirtland Air Force Base, provided by the KAFB Historian," June 2003.

Chapter 25

1. Reed, Ollie, Jr., "KFB Home to Massive Nuclear Storage Complex," *Albuquerque Journal*, April 2016.
2. Kristensen, Hans M., and Matt Korda, "United States Nuclear Forces, 2020," January 2020, https://doi.org/10.1080/00963402.2019.1701286.
3. Kirtland Munitions Decertified, USAF News, February 10, 2010, www.af.mil/news.
4. F.E. Warren Air Force Base, "Commander Outlines Global Strike Command Mission, Vision, Values," www.warren.af.news/article/331982.
5. "Nukes in the Duke City: The Nuclear Weapons Bunker in Albuquerque," July 2017, https://elloborojo.wordpress.com.

Chapter 26

1. Kirtland Air Force Base, Kirtland at Your Service: Pass and Registration, www.kirtland.af.mil/news.
2. McCoy, Brady, Chief Master Sgt., "377th Unveils Renovated Heritage Room, Showcases History of Defenders, 130. Kirtland Air Force Base," www.kirtland.af.mil/news/article/377.
3. Ray, Timothy M., General, Commander Air Force Global Strike Command, FY 20 Posture for Department of Defense Nuclear Forces, May 1, 2019, www.armed-services.senate.gov/info/media/doc/ray.

Chapter Notes

Chapter 27

1. National Security Administration, Final Supplement Analysis, Pantex Plant, November 2012, www.energy.gov./sites/prod/files/EIS-0225-5A.
2. Wolf, Amy F., "The Nuclear Weapons Complex: Overview of Department of Energy Sites," Congressional Research Service, February 2020, https://srsreports.congress.gov.
3. De La Paz, A., "Report on Nuclear Materials Storage—Sandia National Laboratories—New Mexico, June 22, 1994," https://ehss.energy.gov/deprep/1994.
4. Greutman, Michael, "Repurposing and Downgrading of Existing Hazard Category 1, 2, and 3 Nuclear Facilities," March 2017, https://efcog.org/wp-contents/upload/2018104.
5. SNL Nuclear Material initiative/successes, Meeting, May 15, 2017, https://osti.gov/servlets/purl/1457993.
6. O'Brian, Nolan, "LLNL Researchers Salvage Broken Arrow Samples," April 27, 2020, wwwllnl.gov/news.

Epilogue

1. Enjoying Wilderness Areas, https://onda.org/our-approach.

Bibliography

Barkun, Michael. *A Culture of Conspiracy: Apocalyptic Visions in Contemporary America.* Berkeley: University of California Press, May 2006.

Casadel, Greg. *A Gun and Cherries in a Bucket of Blood: The Americanization of an Italian Family and Lessons Learned.* Bloomington: Xlibris, 2014.

Central Intelligence Agency. "The Effect of the Soviet Possibility of Atomic Bombs on the Security of the United States." June 9, 1950.

Deaver, Michael K. *A Different Drummer: My Thirty Years with Ronald Reagan.* New York: HarperCollins, 2001.

Department of Defense Manual, Number 5210.42. "Nuclear Weapons Personnel Reliability Program." January 2015.

Goodwin, Christopher R., and Associates. "Air Force Ammunition and Explosive Storage & Unaccompanied Personnel Housing During the Cold War (1946–1989)." August 2008.

Keeney, Douglas L. *15 Minutes: General Curtis LeMay and the Countdown to Annihilation.* New York: St. Martin's Press, 2011.

Loeber, Charles R. "Building the Bombs: A History of the Nuclear Weapons Complex." Albuquerque: Sandia National Laboratories, 2002.

Page, Joseph T., II "Bombs Away: A Brief 75th Anniversary History of Kirtland Air Force Base." October 2016.

Ray, Timothy M., General, Commander Air Force Global Strike Command. "Presentation to the Senate Armed Services Committee, Subcommittee on Strategic Forces." May 1, 2019.

Robinson, Paul. "Radiation Releases at Sandia National Laboratories/New Mexico." March 2006. 3.

U.S. Department of Commerce, National Technical Information Services. "First History of AFSWP, 1947–1948."

Weitze, Karen J., *Keeping the Edge: Air Force Material Command Cold War Context (1945–1991), Volume II Installations and Facilities* (Headquarters, Air Force Materiel Command, 2003).

Welsh, Michael. "A Mission in the Desert." Albuquerque District, U.S. Army Corp of Engineers.

Wolk, Herman S. "Making the H-Bomb." *Air Force Magazine*, March 2009.

Woolf, Amy F. "The Nuclear Weapons Complex: Overview of Department of Energy, Congressional Research Service." February 2020.

Index

Administrative Area 45, 46, 47, 48, 49, 50, 51, 52, 76, 139, 180
ADT 104, 107, 108, 110, 111, 112, 113, 149, 160, 182, 190
Air Force Global Strike Command 6, 30, 31, 163, 165, 187, 196, 198
Air Force Material Command 19, 31, 161, 193, 198
aircraft crashed at Manzano: B-29 (Superfortress) 10, 28, 60, 107, 135, 136, 175, 182, 195; B-36 (Peacemaker) 28, 60, 84, 128, 135, 137, 147; EC 135 (Air Command) 140, 141, 182; F-100C (Super Saber) 138, 139; Martin/General Dynamics RB-57 140; Navy P-51 140
Alburquerque (original spelling) 6
Amarillo Railroad Museum 126, 127; White Trains 125, 127, 195
Apple Tree 12
Arnold, Henry H. "Hap" 97
Armed Forces Special Weapons Project 1, 11, 17, 19, 22, 27, 29, 40, 190
Army Air Corp (AAC) 27, 190
Army Corp of Engineers 1, 15, 17, 18, 36, 95
Atchison, Topeka and Santa Fe Railroad 7
atomic bomb 6, 9, 10, 13, 14, 16, 17, 18, 21, 28, 34, 37, 57, 58, 62, 63, 71, 79, 135, 137, 146
Atomic Energy Commission (AEC) 11, 14, 15, 16, 17, 18, 19, 22, 29, 34, 35, 37, 40, 46, 54, 55, 63, 64, 75, 77, 78, 82, 84, 90, 118, 151, 164, 192

Bennewitz, Paul (UFO investigator) 148, 149
Birdcage 71, 78, 87, 88, 89, 124, 125
Black and Veatch 34, 38, 67
Broken Arrow 134, 135, 136, 137, 197

Central Security Control Center (CSC) 105, 107, 108, 109, 110, 111, 112, 113, 116, 119, 121, 131, 134, 140, 160, 190
Churchill, Winston (prime minister) 15

Cold War 13, 72, 125, 141, 146, 148, 153, 154, 156, 176, 193, 194, 198
Confederate Army 7
Coyote Canyon 20, 44, 150

Defense Atomic Support Agency (DASA) 1, 19, 20, 22, 23, 46, 48, 157, 185, 190
Department of Defense (DoD) 11, 14, 21, 23, 25, 29, 30, 34, 35, 37, 40, 45, 54, 56, 74, 75, 84, 85, 92, 93, 98, 103, 107, 108, 114, 118, 122, 131, 150, 156, 157, 165, 167, 190, 194, 198
Department of Energy (DoE) 22, 30, 125, 127, 129, 156, 162, 164, 172, 174, 175, 186, 190, 192, 193, 195, 197
disarmament negotiations and treaties 154, 155, 196
Domenici, Pete (NM senator) 162
Doolittle, Jimmy 28

Eisenhower, Dwight 19, 57, 152, 153, 157, 196

Four Hills Ranch 12, 13, 144

Gorbachev, Mikhail 153
Greenglass, David (Soviet spy) 10, 13, 58
Groves, Lesslie 11, 15, 16, 18, 39, 40, 192

Hackett, Frank 8
Hannis Henry F. 35
Heritage Room 169, 170
Hiroshima, Japan 9, 16, 18, 28, 37, 64, 137, 138
Historic District, Manzano MSA 175

Kennedy, John 152, 153, 169, 192, 195
Kirtland, Roy C. 9, 27, 193
Kirtland Air Force Base 6, 23, 26, 27, 28, 29, 30, 31, 44, 101, 148, 150, 158, 161, 185, 189, 190, 193, 196
Kirtland Army Air Field 9, 14, 27, 28, 40
Kirtland Underground Munitions Maintenance and Storage Complex (KUMMSC) 160, 162, 167, 186

Index

Lawrence Livermore National Laboratory 175
LeMay, Curtis E. 97, 192, 193, 198
Los Alamos National Laboratory (LANL) 9, 10, 90, 146, 151, 162, 173

Manhattan Project 1, 9, 10, 11, 14, 15, 16, 17, 18, 21, 39, 96, 98, 183
Manzano Mountain Range 12, 13, 35, 44, 66, 134, 138, 139, 140, 141, 144, 148, 183, 192

Nagasaki, Japan 9, 13, 16. 18, 28, 39
National Nuclear Security Administration (NNSA) 90, 129, 130, 173, 191, 195
National Register of Historic Places 175
Nixon, Richard 157, 185
nuclear weapons at Manzano: Fat Man 13, 37, 39, 57, 59, 80, 81, 88, 184; Hydrogen 60, 63, 64, 72, 137; Little Boy 64, 81, 137; Mark (MK) 3 37, 39, 57, 59, 80, 81, 184; Mark (MK) 4 37, 40, 62; Mark (MK) 5 60, 184, 194; Mark (MK) 6 60, 61, 184; Mark (MK) 12 62; Mark (MK) 17 63, 194; Mark (MK) 18 60, 61; Mark (MK) 24 64; thermonuclear 14, 60, 61, 62, 63, 64, 72, 76, 78, 79, 83, 128, 137, 152, 184
Nuclear Weapons Security Program 18, 45, 56, 74, 92, 93, 96, 157
Nuclear Weapons storage sites: Lake Mead Base, Nevada 37; Medina Base, Texas 37; Site Able, Albuquerque, NM 1, 2, 11, 18, 19, 34, 35, 37, 38, 39, 40, 41, 98, 99, 183, 184; Site Baker, Killeen, Texas 37, 38, 40, 50, 99, 157, 161; Site Charlie, Kentucky 37; Site Dog, Bossier Base, LA 37
nuclear weapons storage structures (bunkers) 20, 44, 55, 66, 67, 68, 69, 71, 73, 141, 149, 159, 160, 173, 174, 182, 184, 185, 186; Type A 71,72, 88, 194; Type B 68, 69, 194; Type C 70, 194; Type D 70, 71, 194; Type S 72, 194

Office of Scientific Research and Development 15
Operation Sandstone 39, 40, 193
Oppenheimer, Robert (SNL director) 9, 21, 62
Oxnard, James G. 8
Oxnard Field 8, 11, 18, 21, 183

Pantex Plant, Texas 172, 197
Pass and Badge Office, Manzano 45, 46, 48
Personal Reliability Program (PRP) 75
Personnel Security Questionnaire 65, 75
PIT (Capsule) 60, 61, 72, 87, 88, 89, 90, 124, 128, 135, 172, 173
power generator backup 112

Presidential Emergency Facility (PEF) 85
Project Water Supply 34, 35, 183
Pueblo Indians 12

R. Christopher Goodwin & Associates (RCG&A) 71, 77, 79, 87, 111
radiation 24, 82, 83, 88, 89, 140, 174, 193, 198
railhead 44, 124, 130
Ray, Timothy M. 31 171, 193, 196, 198
Reagan, Ronald 153, 196, 198
Rocky Flats Plant, Denver 90, 173
Roosevelt, Franklin 14, 15

Saddle Road 119, 140
safe, secure railcars (SSRs) 125
Sandia Base 1, 2, 6, 11, 12, 14, 18, 19, 20, 21, 22, 23, 25, 27, 29, 34, 35, 37, 39, 40, 44, 48, 49, 50, 76, 82, 99, 115, 122, 124, 130, 146, 147,150, 157, 158, 183,184, 185, 193
Sandia National Laboratories (SNL) 23, 24, 25, 34, 102, 108, 161, 168, 172, 174, 175, 176, 186, 187, 191, 197
Security Police at Manzano: Manhattan District Military Police 98, 99; 8455th Military Police Company 40, 50, 95, 98; 4900th Security Police Squadron 100, 105, 159, 160, 167; 1094th Air Police Squadron 19, 41, 55, 99, 100, 111, 112, 114, 118, 119, 121, 124, 125, 128, 130, 132, 143, 145, 159, 160, 184, 185, 188; Sandia National Laboratories Security 102, 172; 1606/1608 Security Police Squadron 30, 78, 98, 100, 101, 112, 117, 141, 160, 167, 186, 195; 377th Security Forces Group 30, 101,102, 105, 107, 117, 120, 132, 161, 163, 167, 168, 169, 170, 171, 172, 175, 186, 187, 189, 192, 196
Sibley, Henry Hopkins 7
Strategic Air Command 14, 45, 63, 81, 97, 100, 141

teenager electrocution 106, 195
tickling the tiger's tail 89
top-secret security clearance 74
Transportation and Safeguards Division 129
Truman, Harry 14, 34, 54, 156

unidentified flying object (UFO) 35, 146, 147 148, 149, 150, 151, 196; Bennewitz, Paul (UFO investigator) 148, 149; Dulce Base 148–149
USAF Project Blue Book 148

weapons maintenance plants 37, 38, 74, 75, 77, 79, 81, 83, 85, 112, 122, 159, 184; Plant Number I 74,76, 77, 78, 81, 86, 88, 185;

Index

Plant Number II 70, 74, 76, 77, 78, 86, 160, 184, 185; Plant Number III 64, 78, 79, 81, 83, 195; Plant Number IV 78, 79, 184, 195

Yeltsin, Boris 153, 154

Z Division 18, 21, 183

www.ingramcontent.com/pod-product-compliance
Ingram Content Group UK Ltd.
Pitfield, Milton Keynes, MK11 3LW, UK
UKHW042005140426
5217IPUK00015B/998